Acclaim for Monica Anderson

"The quality our readers like best about Monica's column is that they see themselves through her writing. Monica has a special talent for taking the events of daily life and turning them into adventures. She seems to have endless material with which to delight readers. She evokes readers' emotions that range from a knowing smile to belly laughs and tears. You're going to love her work."

~ Wes Turner, President and Publisher,
Fort Worth Star-Telegram

"Monica Anderson has a refreshing way of capturing the ironic twists of everyday family life with a big dose of humor. Her words tickle our hearts and bring laughter to our souls."

~ Ramona Logan,
Anchor, KXAS TV 5

"It is a special kind of columnist who writes with power, yet sensitivity, with humor, yet with profound poignancy, with flair, yet simplicity. Monica Anderson is a special kind of writer."

~ Bob Ray Sanders,
Fort Worth Star-Telegram

"The late great Erma Bombeck died in 1996, but fans of the SuperMom genre of columnists didn't miss a beat., That same year, Monica Anderson began tickling her readers with Erma's eternal truth!"

~ Dave Lieber, secretary,
National Society of Newspaper Columnists

"... Anderson is the best of the lot. Kind of a '90s version of Erma Bombeck, she writes about the joys and foibles of parenthood, work and modern life in a way that causes you to nod your head in recognition. And she does it without an ounce of self-righteousness, condescension or sappiness."

~Fort Worth Weekly, September 16-23, 1999, whose staff
Selected Monica Anderson as "Best Newspaper Columnist"

"This is perfect, the kind of material that people enjoy reading ~ a very nice flare to it and original to boot. I loved it"

~ Betty Wright, Publisher,
Rainbook Books, Inc.

"I get so much pleasure from reading Monica Anderson. Not only are her columns thought-provoking, they are inspiring, entertaining and so true-to-life."

~ Cheryl Smith
KKDA-AM

Diane,
Best Wishes!

Mom, Are We There Yet?

Selected Columns
by
Monica F. Anderson

Illustrations by Mark Fields

Dream A Little Inc.
Louisville, Kentucky

Published by Dream A Little Inc.
Louisville, Kentucky 40207

All columns are reprinted
with the permission of the Fort Worth Star-Telegram
and/or Arlington Star-Telegram
which hold the exclusive rights to them.

Illustrations by Mark Fields

ISBN 0-9662703-2-0
Library of congress Catalog Card Number: 00-133358

Dedication

To the memory of my grandmothers:

Ruby Tucker Frazier
Marshall, Texas
1899-1987

Lucile Johnson Henry
Jefferson, Texas
1910-1996

Edith Roberson Jenkins
Overton, Texas
1913-1998

Acknowledgments

As always, to God be the glory for the things He has done.

One of my many blessings is my family; my husband, Alfred, and my two sons (names withheld to protect the innocent). Thank you guys for your patience, support and encouragement while Mom tries to juggle all these balls. A special thank you also, to my mom & dad, Gladys and Jimmy Jenkins. Little sister, J. Chase, you're the best sister I've ever had!

Rochelle Riley, editor, publisher, friend - I couldn't have done this without you. Thanks a million.

Mark Fields, thank you for the wonderful illustrations and for believing in me and this dream of mine.

I also want to acknowledge my Star-Telegram colleagues, especially, Ashley Cheshire, Gary Hardee and Jim Witt.

I owe a debt of gratitude to the wonderful folks that gave me testimonials: Judge Tom Vandergriff, Wesley R. Turner, Ruby Odom, Ramona Logan, Bob Ray Sanders, William Dwight McKissic, Sr., Theresa Hartley, Cheryl Smith, Dave Lieber, and Betty Wright.

I have so many wonderful friends and family members who have contributed to this project in ways great and small. I appreciate every idea, every note of encouragement, every call to say that I made you laugh and every act of kindness that you've shown my family.

I can't possibly name all of you but I'm going to list as many as I can: Karen Kennard, Sophia Williams (my right hand), Scott Joslove, Yvonne Gilliam ~ my publicist, Lawrence and Margie Young, the members of Soul Sisters Literary Discussion Group, my Greek family ~ Zeta Phi Beta Sorority and Phi Beta Sigma Fraternity, La Mad Writers Group, Ron Wright, Dr. Ken Wallace (Thanks for covering for me all those times), Dr. Clay Ellis, Gloria Kennard (Thank goodness you saved all those columns Auntie!), Vanessa Wesley, Larry Lias, Charles (Webmaster) Harris, my church family at Cornerstone Baptist Church, Pastor Daniels and Pilgrim

Valley Baptist Church, my wonderful patients who've been so understanding about my crazy schedule, ALL of my family: Johnsons, Henrys, Fraziers, Buchanans, Jenkins, Chases, Grays, Haliburtons, Andersons, Halls… (I can't name all 10 zillion of you guys but I love you.)

I would be remiss if I didn't thank all of the groups, organizations, clubs and corporations that have invited me to speak. I used feedback from those engagements, along with the numerous voice mails and letters received from readers to select these particular columns for publication.

Finally, better late than never, a big thank you to all of the bookstores, radio stations, newspapers and magazines that featured me when I was promoting my previous book. It's out of print but you'll always be in my heart. Just one more list, guys. I've got to mention some of these folks and book stores because they went out of their way to give a forum to an unknown writer.

A super big thank you to: Sonia and Elvis at the Black Book Worm, Emma Rodgers at Black Images Books, Barnes and Noble, B. Dalton, Borders Books, Willis Johnson, Jokaes, The Dallas Weekly, The Dallas Morning News, KKDA, Doug Banks, Tavis Smiley, Sandra Daniels, Good Morning Texas and everybody else that just spelled my name right!

Thank you all very, very much.

Smooches,
Monica

Contents

Mom, Are We
There Yet?

Mom, Are We There Yet?

There's nothing like a family road trip to make you appreciate the Wright Brothers. Surely, they came up with the idea for a flying machine after taking a long car trip with their young children.

My husband and I, along with the boys, Peat and Repeat, went to visit my aunt and uncle last weekend. I carefully plotted our course on the map so that we would take the shortest possible route between our house and theirs. We brought along pillows and blankets for napping. There was a sack full of snacks tucked in the trunk next to the cooler. Dad had the car finely tuned and filled with unleaded gasoline.

The boys had an assortment of audiotapes and several games to keep them amused during the drive and I gave the boys the routine lecture before we got into the car.

"Boys, go to the restroom now. If you don't need to go, force yourself to go. We will not stop every five minutes for restroom breaks. You cannot have a snack until we are beyond the city limits. Do not touch each other. Stay on your side of the seat. Do not lick the windows or kick the back of my seat. And most importantly, do not ask, 'Are we there yet?' When we pull into Uncle Rayford's driveway, we are there. OK? Does everyone understand?"

The boys nodded, but I could see my futile words swarming around their dirty little ears looking in vain for a small entrance into their heads.

We were a block from home when Peat said, "Mom, I'm thirsty." I broke my last Tic Tac in half and gave each of them a piece.

We were one mile from home when Repeat announced, "I have to go the restroom."

I gave him a withering look but he didn't wither. He wiggled instead. Every parent knows that wiggle. It means: "We have one minute 'til blast off. Stop the car now!"

When we stopped at the service station, Repeat said, "Are we

there yet? Is this Uncle Rayford's house?"
We didn't answer so he said, "I'm hungry. Can I have a snack?"

We were not even out of our neighborhood yet and my head was starting to throb. Once we reached the freeway, I suggested a game. No one wanted to play a game. I tried to start a conversation. No one would talk to me. So I retrieved my novel from my purse and started this new book that I'd been itching to read. As soon as I creased the cover, they decided they wanted to talk to me.

"Mom, what are transmissions made out of?"

"I have no idea. Ask your father," I said, struggling to concentrate.

"Mom, is that a dead raccoon or a dead possum over there in the street?"

I glanced at the mass of matter and guessed, "It's a dead armadillo."

"Mom, did you ever eat an armadillo?"

I sighed. "No, but I've eaten raccoon and possum. Of course, there was that mystery meat back in high school, but to my knowledge, I have not eaten armadillo."

"Mom, if a raccoon and a possum had a fight, who would win?"

"Raccoons and possums don't fight. They are cousins. And please don't fight with your cousins at Uncle Rayford's house."

"But what if they got mad at each other - like, really mad."
"They would ask an armadillo to help them settle the argument with mediation and binding arbitration."

"Does that mean that they kill him and throw him in the street?"
"Yes."

A few minutes later, as I turned to Page 4, the boys started punching each other. I yelled, "Stop it! I don't care what happened or who started it!" I never looked up from my book because I really didn't care what happened or who started it. I just wanted peace and quiet. I was fairly certain that we would never reach our destination.

During the entire trip, my husband uttered two words, "Good grief!" He said good grief every time we stopped for a potty break. In 30 minutes, we stopped three times. During one of these side trips, I noticed that Repeat was not wearing shoes. He forgot. He didn't have any holes in his socks, though.

Listen, when we finally reached Uncle Rayford's house in Fort Worth, 20 miles away from our house, no one was more relieved than me.

I'd Rather Have A Puppy

My sons, Clem and Jim, get along real well for about nine hours out of every day. The other 15 hours, when they're awake, they fight like cats and dogs.

They argue about everything from who gets to sit in the front seat of the car to who gets the last slice of pizza. They're fiercely competitive. If I say three words to one of them, I have to say exactly three words to the other one ~ not a word more or less.

Frankly, it drives me crazy. I have a much younger sister. We had a good arrangement. I was right about everything, and she was born to do my bidding. I guess I should have spaced my kids further apart ~ like 18 or 20 years.

I should have known there was going to be trouble the day we brought little Jim home from the hospital. Clem greeted us at the door wearing a cowboy hat and pointing a toy pistol at us. We didn't buy him the gun; he made it himself out of Legos.

"He can't come in here," he said, waving the red-blue-and-yellow six shooter at the tiny bundle in my arms.

"Oh sweetie," I said. "This is your little brother. We've been looking forward to him coming home. Remember, we've talked about it for months. He's going to be your special baby."

I tried to walk past three-year-old Clem but he spread his arms and stubby legs and refused to budge.

"I don't want him. Take him back," he ordered, frowning ferociously.

"Honey, he's your baby. We promised you a little baby brother and here he is ~ see, he looks just like you," I said, folding the blanket back to reveal the baby's angelic face.

Clem wasn't impressed. "He don't look like me. He don't have no hair. He's ugly."

I looked to my husband for help.

"Son," he said, "this is the most special day in the world. You'll remember this day forever. This is the day you get someone to play with, someone to be your best friend for the rest of your life."

"I wanted a puppy. I can play with a puppy. A puppy is my friend. A puppy gots hair."

As the days passed, I became anxious for the baby. His brother developed an intense fascination with the soft spot in the center of his head. He insisted on touching it all of the time. Sometimes he pushed so hard, I thought he was trying to skewer Jim's little brain. Eventually, we bought Jim a helmet that also came in handy all those times Clem accidentally dropped him.

We did everything we could to help Clem accept and learn to love his little brother. We gave him lots of special attention and made sure that our friends didn't ignore him when they came over to see the new baby. But Clem just wasn't impressed with his new friend.

One day I went into the nursery, and Clem was standing next to his brother's crib just glaring at him.

"What's wrong honey?" I inquired.

"He can't do anything. He's no good. Take him back to the stork store. Get us another brother that can play."

"Honey, he'll grow up real soon. You couldn't do much when you were his age but look at what a big boy you are now. You'll just have to teach him how to do things. That's a big brother's job you know."

Eureeka! I finally hit the nail on the head.

Assigned the job of teaching his little brother the ropes, Clem got a totally new attitude. Thankfully, his brother worshipped the ground he walked on for the first few years. All we had to do was keep the crayons locked up so they wouldn't write their ABC's on the wall again, and things went smoothly for a good while.

Then it happened: Jim got a mind of his own.

He got fed up with being a servant and started asserting himself. Not only would he not follow his brother's orders, he would do exactly the opposite of whatever his brother suggested. It's been chaos around here every since. From Sunday school to child psychology, I've tried everything to teach those two to love and respect each other. Most of the time I feel like I'm plowing whipped cream.

My husband says this is normal ~ that he and his brothers were the same way. I remind him that they haven't changed either. They still tease each other. He says that's the way men show love.

Yesterday, I was working in the yard as my boys played hockey in the street with some neighborhood kids. Jim was driving towards the goal when he collided with Mikey, and both boys went crashing to the ground. Before I could react, Clem went over and helped his brother up; then both boys helped Mikey. I smiled to myself. "That's the way you show love," I thought.

Two minutes later, my sons were hitting each other with their hockey sticks.

Is it too late to take them both back to the stork store?

Baby's Got His Blue Jeans On

The phone rings. Briiinggg. I answer.

All she actually says is, *"Hi. Is Alfred home?"* But what I hear is, Hi. Ha. Ha. It's 10 o'clock at night and I'm calling to steal your husband. I'm a perky, eighteen-year-old, volleyball player with a Ferrari and implants. I spend every waking hour plotting to break up your marriage. I'm calling to make him an offer he can't refuse. *"Is Alfred home?"* I'm letting you have him for one more night, but then he's all mine. Now hand over the phone, loser."

Yes, jealousy is an ugly thing. I've always prided myself on being the secure, self-confident type. I've studiously avoided the dreaded where've-you-beens and secret-wallet searches. In return, my husband doesn't give me a hard time about having lunch with a male colleague or going out for a night on the town with the girls. We're not even close to perfect, but we've found something that works for us.

Sure, I got a little bent out of shape that time, years ago, when his bowling partner, the cheerleader, wore her uniform to bowling class. Who could let that pass without comment? He said that he didn't even notice her, and I was making a big deal out of nothing. Maybe I did overreact, but the team didn't even have a game that day. Furthermore, she wasn't even a real cheerleader; she just liked the outfit.

So, like I said, I've mostly resisted my obsessive, compulsive urges–until recently.

Blame those blue jeans.

Everyone has a perfect pair of blue jeans waiting for them some-where in the universe. You know, the ones that look as if they were custom-made for your body. But, it's easier to find a soul mate than that ideal piece of denim. Most of us spend years vainly shopping for that one glorious piece of apparel. We may come close but usu-ally the waist is a little big or they fit funny around the hips.

You know you've hit pay dirt when they fit you just right from waist to ankle without being so tight in some places that they're disgusting. If at least one out of every four heads turns to check you out when you walk by, you've found THE jeans.

My husband found HIS jeans last month. Every since then, I've been a bundle of nerves. When we go to the grocery store, I walk right behind him to block the view. Two women crashed their carts head-on last week when I briefly ventured off to weigh some fruit. I hate those jeans. I've asked him not to wear them outside our home but he just laughs at me.

Now this strange woman is calling in the middle of the night. I know she's seen his jeans. I hand him the phone and linger nearby to sort out the junk mail.

He says, "Hello?" Then I wait anxiously through five minutes of, "Uh huh. Yes. Uh huh."

Finally, he tells her, "We're very happy with our long distance carrier but thank you for calling."

He hangs up and asks me, "Moe, why did you just throw all of our bills into the trash can?"

What can I say? It's the jeans.

Be Specific With Kids

After you spend a lot of time with a person, you begin to understand them. Observing their actions and reactions to various situations gives one a certain assurance. You acquire almost a psychic ability to predict their behavior. And there is some comfort in knowing that, good, bad, or ugly, consistency reigns. If I do A, then I'm 99 percent sure that B will happen. Of course, all of this makes it easier to decide which voice in your head to listen to. You do hear voices, too, don't you?

Then one day something happens to make you question everything you know. The world stops spinning, and the sun rises in the west. Everyone else has something to hold on to when gravity ceases to be, but you go flying off into the horizon like a space shuttle without a map. Know what I mean?

Take the other day for instance. We're preparing for an early morning outing and I yell to the kids, "Turn off the television and get dressed! We have to leave in 30 minutes."

I know that they will not turn off the television immediately. They will pretend that they didn't hear me. I just want to plant that seed in their little minds hoping it will grow into a thought during a commercial break.

Five minutes later, I say, "Turn that television off now! Get dressed. It is 100 degrees outside. Do not put on your new fall school clothes. Put on some old shorts and a T-shirt."

I hear them mumbling something kind about me as they turn off the television reluctantly. Three minutes later, my youngest son is downstairs dressed and ready to go. Indeed he's wearing some old shorts and a faded T-shirt as instructed. They appear to be clean. However, something is amiss.

"Son, did you brush your teeth and hair?" I ask, knowing the answer already.

"No," he says innocently and raises his eyebrows in surprise.

"Why not?"

"You didn't tell me to. You just said to get dressed."

Exasperated, I respond, "Son, for over a decade now I've given you the same instructions every morning. 'Get up, make your bed, brush your teeth, wash your face and ears, and put on clean clothes.' Now how many times do I have to say that before you remember?"

"I don't know."

You must be specific with children. Giving them directions is like playing "Simon Says". They will only do exactly what "Simon" says and if "Simon" doesn't say it, well, it's not happening.

I try logic.

"Sweetie, why should you brush your teeth everyday?"

He stands on one foot and looks at the ceiling earnestly pondering.

"Because you tell us too?" he offers hopefully.

"No, because of the germs. Remember?"

"Oh yeah, cavities."

"Exactly. The germs are there every morning and every night. You have to kill them before they hurt your teeth. I shouldn't have to remind you everyday. Just do it, OK? It's your job to keep your body clean so it smells good and feels good. Now go brush your teeth and while you're at it, do something with your hair please."

"OK."

Shortly afterwards, his brother comes along looking halfway presentable. "Son, did you do everything: Hair? Teeth? Make your bed?"

"Yes ma'am."

This is too good to be true. I give him the once over and inquire, "Did you change underwear?"

"We're supposed to change our underwear, too?"

See what I mean?

Crumbs On The Floor

Last night I cooked tuna fish sandwiches and potato chips. OK, no cooking was involved but I took several minutes to artistically arrange the food on clean plates and cut the sandwiches in half. Then I put the plates right in the middle of the kitchen floor and called my family to dinner.

Footsteps echoed through the house as they responded to the good news.

Now, sometimes I put the tuna on a lettuce leaf. No one actually eats the lettuce but it seems like a more nutritious meal if I do that. It's more colorful, too. Meat and vegetables, you know. However, my friend Karen has informed me that fish and chicken are not meat. They are fish and poultry, respectively. She's a lawyer so she knows these things. Anyway, my son says that there are five food groups now instead of four like I was taught back in the Stone Age. Maybe the fifth group is tuna.

So my family waltzes in, and they have the nerve to look surprised like they've never seen food on the floor before.

"What's going on mom?" they ask in a tone of bewilderment.

"Well sweetie, I just thought I'd save the crumbs the trouble of leaping from the table to their certain death on the tile below. This way they can just climb over the edge of the plate and wait with their friends until I sweep the floor after dinner."

Come to think of it, they probably haven't seen the buffet of food they leave around the table. They lean so far back in their chairs that sometimes I'm tempted to get them a footstool. Every crumb falls on their shirts or the floor. I really do need to start letting them share in the joy of sweeping more often.

"That's crazy mom."

They tell me that a lot.

"Parents inherit craziness from their children," I reply with a twisted smile.

I just want my kitchen to stay clean for five minutes. If you must get a glass of water, wait for five minutes after I finish washing dishes. Don't get one of the glasses that I just washed; get a new glass. A dry glass. And if you really want to make my top spin, just cup your hand under the faucet and drink. But please don't drip any water on the floor that I just swept. Five minutes that's all I ask.

Moms are weird about these things. We are constantly surrounded by chaos. Kids are running in and out. The phone is ringing off the hook. The television doesn't stay on one channel long enough to watch a commercial. We've got more bills on the counter than food in the fridge. In the midst of all this commotion, we need some stability, however fleeting. No, nothing as unlikely as dinner at the same time each night with everyone present. That would be a miracle.

All we ask for is a bag of cookies that lasts longer than a day or flushed toilets with the seat down. Perhaps even a hint that we're out of milk before we pour ourselves a bowl of cereal on Saturday morning.

Go ahead. Call me a dreamer. But what kind of awful world would this be without dreamers and their beautiful kids that drop crumbs on clean floors? Yes, they must and they will learn about being considerate and demonstrating good table manners.

But the kids will grow up and leave. The floor will be there long after the last crumb is gone.

Birds & Bees

Every parent looks forward to sharing certain events with their children.

After our kids were born, we eagerly anticipated the moments when they would learn to crawl and say "da-da" or "ma-ma."

Actually, I was pushing that "da-da" phrase pretty hard. Whenever my husband wasn't home, I would chant "da-da" to the boys over and over. Then, at 3 AM, when the glorious tune of "da-da" came sailing through the baby monitor, I could honestly say to him, "Your son is calling you."

We rejoiced when our sons started to stand on their chubby, unsteady legs and pull everything off the coffee table. Eventually, I started to prefer magazines with the covers torn off. We have hours and hours of videotape capturing the exhilarating "firsts" in their lives. We filmed the first tooth for an hour.

We spent evening after evening in the street teaching them to ride a bike. Their Dad gave them helmets and let them go for it after a couple of lessons. I continued to hold on to the seat of the bike and run behind them even after it was obvious that they didn't need my help anymore.

It's hard to let go when you know what could happen.

Yes, we've joyfully celebrated numerous milestones of their growing independence and maturity. And then it happened. That moment every parent dreads and avoids came hurdling into our home and knocked me for a loop. Little Dustin asked me, "Where do babies come from?"

Ai yi yi!!!!

I should have seen it coming. Little signs of puberty poking from Dustin's legs and arms in the form of dark, curly hairs where baby smooth skin used to be. I could smell it in the ferocious odor oozing from his brother's underarms when he forgets to apply deodorant. I've watched their innocence be plucked from their mouths with each frequent visit of the tooth fairy.

They say, "fools rush in where wise (wo)men never go." So I

waited and watched as we talked about anatomy and the proper terms for body parts. On some issues, I've been very specific. Dustin already knew where babies come from; what he really wanted to know was how the baby got there in the first place. I've been quite vague about that subject. In other words, he had all of the game pieces; he just didn't know the rules.

My spouse and I were forced to deal with this sensitive subject by two recent events. First, we learned that my eldest boy would soon be shown "the video" in P.E. You know the one that talks about the differences between boys and girls and why they have every reason to hate each other.   As I recall, it doesn't get too graphic or detailed, which is good. But it does set those little minds to wondering. I just didn't want him to be as surprised as I was when I saw the video many moons ago.

My poor mother hadn't told me anything. The film left me more perplexed than ever. Thank goodness for "National Geographic" and the encyclopedia. By the time my Mom got around to talking to me, I was in the eighth grade. I could have told her some stuff by then. (Things I'd gleaned from my extensive reading, of course.)

The second event that heralded the day of reckoning was a conversation I overheard one day when I was washing dishes and my boys were lying on the floor and watching television.

"Justin, are you ever going to have kids?" Dustin asked his older brother.

He quickly responded, "No way, man! I hate girls! I'm never gonna get married so I'll never have any kids."

I must say that I was pleased with his response. My smile soon evaporated, however.

Justin continued, "Dustin, you better never, ever kiss a girl, because that's how you make babies."

Dustin, my baby, corrected his big brother. "No, you have to lay on them while you kiss them to make a baby."

I started choking on the air and they both turned to watch me sputter and wheeze. The room started spinning and my heartbeat became irregular.

As soon as I heard my husband's car in the driveway that

evening, I rushed to the door to tell him about the boy's discussion. We agreed that it was indeed time for THE TALK.

I tried to persuade him that it was his responsibility since we have boys. They could go out behind the swing set and have a big heart to heart. He thought I should do it because of my medical background. I don't even think so.

We compromised. We went to the video store and rented "What's Happening to Me?" a neat video about puberty, and "Where Do Babies Come From," a horror movie for shy parents. Y'all, it was the best we could do. I'd like to say that we sat down at the dining table with an anatomy book and had a round table discussion, but we're parents of the new millenium. We did watch the videos alone first to ensure that they were age appropriate and accurate.

They were outstanding. Much more thorough and entertaining than the two of us alone could have ever been. The following evening, we brought the boys into the den and explained what we were going to see and why. They protested. We sweated.

I barely survived the puberty video. I was so embarrassed that I looked like a beet. My husband and I didn't blink or move the entire time. Afterwards, we discussed the movie- sort of. They didn't have any questions or comments. Thank goodness.

Then, my husband switched videos, and I panicked. I couldn't make it through the opening credits showing the mommy and daddy hugging.

"I'm going in the other room," I announced, "This is a father/son thing." I ran into my bedroom before my husband could stop me.

When the video ended, I returned to the den.

"Boys, do you have any questions?" I asked in a tone of voice that indicated I would prefer that they not ask me anything. They just stared at me. Dustin looked disgusted. I felt like my pedestal had been shattered, and I was now just a girl in their eyes.

"Well, you can ask me anything at anytime. OK? I want you to come to me or Dad and not your friends whenever you need to know more about any of these things. Don't ask your friends because they don't know anymore than you do."

They just kept staring at me. Finally, Dustin said, "Mom, did you do that when you got pregnant with me and Justin?"

I'm sure I had a heart attack but unfortunately I didn't die. I looked at my husband with the anguished expression of a gold fish in a plastic bag riding the roller coaster at Six Flags.

"Boys," I said, "do you remember the story of Mary and Joseph in the Bible?"

"Yes."

"Um, now wasn't that a wonderful story? I love that story even though it happened thousands of years ago. And you know, nothing like that has ever happened again."

Their puzzled expressions were comforting. "In fact, I'm going to go read that story again right now. Does anyone want to hear a Bible story?"

"No," they replied in unison.

"OK then, I'll be in my room if you need me."

As I closed the bedroom door, I could feel those invisible apron strings stretch and grow taut. I let out a little more line as though I was flying a kite on a windy day. Someday, I'll cut those strings and let my children fly away into the horizon like every mother has to do sooner or later. But for now, I'm holding on with both hands.

It's hard to let go when you know what could happen.

Girls Are Sorry

On a chilly Saturday morning last fall, I arose at dawn, hung new cabinet doors in the master bathroom, painted the kids' tree house and mowed the lawn before cooking breakfast for my family.

After cleaning up the kitchen, I was shampooing the carpet when the phone rang. It was a call for my youngest son. I missed most of the conversation because I was lifting the love seat to clean beneath it, but when I paused to catch my breath, I heard him say: "I know. Girls are sorry. All they can do is cook and be cheerleaders."

My head rotated 360 degrees around the pulsating veins in my neck and it wasn't just because of all the hardworking, talented cheerleaders that he'd offended with that chauvinistic remark. In that eerily calm voice that women use when they're about to go ballistic, I asked him, "Sweetheart, what did you just say?"

I didn't even wait for an answer.

"Son, didn't you see me change the brake pads on the truck yesterday all by myself? And can't I spit farther than any boy at your school? And didn't I just run you and your father all up and down the basketball court while pumping in seven three-pointers from half court? Is that sorry, mister?"

I could not believe that my son, the child of Ms. Dr. Monica Frazier Anderson, had uttered those profane words. Wherever did I go wrong?

"Well mom, you can't beat me at football," he declared, smiling through the perfect teeth that I clean for free every six months. "Girls are no good at football."

My husband is an avid football fan. Naturally, my son associates football with males. That is fine ~ football, hunting, burping out loud, scratching in public ~ men things. Okay. No problem. But "girls are sorry" is just a bit too much.

I quickly rallied the other mothers. A challenge was issued. Wednesday, 4 PM, the playground. Flag football. Moms vs Boys. Be There!

And there we were, the boys, most of them missing teeth, wearing shorts and jerseys. And the mothers, who weren't all that familiar with flag football, attaching the long, yellow flags to their belts with safety pins instead of Velcro.

It started out like a dream. The Mighty Moms scored four touchdowns in a row. Only three of us had ever played football in our lives, and we delighted in mentioning that fact every time we ran a play. Then it happened. The little boys started pouting and whining. One fellow even cried. The moms called a huddle.

"Let them win. It's no big deal," suggested the crying kid's mother. "We don't want to injure their self-esteem."

"Go to the sideline and be a cheerleader," we told her.

"Well, just let them score a few points."

We could agree to that. On the next play from scrimmage, we fell all over each other, and the boys reached the goal line. They were ecstatic, leaping up and down, and passing out high fives as if they'd won the Super Bowl.

A minute later we came to the final play of the game. The moms had possession and we had planned to simply run out the clock and then pass out the fresh, baked chocolate chip cookies. But just before the snap, one of the boys yelled: "They're just big girls! Girls suck! Boys rule! We can stop them!"

Ooh, he shouldn't have said that.

The quarterback took the snap and handed the ball off to me. My injured self-esteem rose with every step as I left my size nine footprints all over those dudes. Eighty yards and a touchdown later, I felt mighty good.

The following day, as I adjusted my neck brace and soaked my feet in Epsom Salt, my son ventured, "Mom, my friends said that you're really fast."

"Oh really?" I commented with a satisfied smile.

"Yeah, but I told them that my Dad is way faster than you."

Summer Is Too Expensive

Let's just cancel this season. Summer vacation is not working out. My children have only been out of school for only two weeks and I think that is about long enough.

It's not that I don't enjoy their company, to the contrary, every moment is special. It's just that I feel selfish having them all to myself for hours and hours everyday. Other people deserve to share in the joy, the camaraderie, the electric bill.

Frankly, I can't afford summer. My children think we're supposed to do something exciting and entertaining every single day. They become bored right after breakfast. We've got 2,000 channels of television but they can't find a single program worth watching or a book that will hold their interest. I barely get a cup of coffee down before the whining starts.

"Mom, can we turn the air conditioner on? It's hot in here."

"It is on."

"But Mom, look at all the sweat on my face. I'm burning up."

"That's not sweat, it's dew. You woke up too early. Just sit still and breathe slowly."

In disbelief, my son walks over to the thermostat and exclaims, "This thing is on 78 degrees! Can I turn it down some? It's cooler outside than it is in here."

"If you do, we'll have to unplug the refrigerator. Take your choice. It doesn't matter to me. You and your brother have eaten up all the food anyway. Which reminds me, please stop leaving empty boxes in the pantry and also, whenever there is only one potato chip left, feel free to dispose of the bag."

"Man, you and Dad are so cheap."

"No, cheap people don't want to spend their money. We are simply broke. We want to spend money but we don't have any because we spent it all on Star Wars, Putt Putt, football camp, seven trips to the grocery store, new swimming trunks, goggles and T-shirts."

He remains unfazed by our plight.

"Hey, my old T-shirts had holes in the armpits."

"And? Just keep your arms down. Forget basketball; play hockey."

"OK, what about our allowance? We haven't gotten it for two weeks."

"There are twelve pennies in a box under my bed. I was saving them for a special occasion but you can split them with your brother. I'll just cut my hair my self."

Laughing, he says, "Gee, you're worse than Ebenezer Scrooge."

"Son, Ebenezer had money. I'm just broke. Now, go put your goggles on, it will keep that dew out of your eyes."

Dining Out With Kids

Eating at a restaurant was a big deal when I was a kid. We had a limited budget and just a few dining establishments to choose from.

There was the cafeteria that we only went to on Sunday after church. There were a couple of hamburger places that took forever to make a burger but they made it just the way we liked it, well done and juicy. Then there was the chicken place that also sold fried fish that tasted like chicken or maybe the chicken tasted like fish. And finally, there was the barbecue place that used to have a dog outside but the dog disappeared the day they added sausage to the menu.

Most of the time, however, we ate at home. Dad would throw something on the grill or Mom would fry up some pork chops that tasted like fried chicken. When we did eat out, I never complained about the location or the menu.

But with these Y2Kids, it's a totally different story. Eating at a restaurant to them is as routine as riding a bike to a friend's house but a lot more complicated. The confusion starts the moment we leave home in search of nourishment.

"What do you guys want to eat?" I ask foolishly.

"Let's get hamburgers," suggests Child One.

"I'm tired of hamburgers," Child Two whines, "I want pizza."

"We just had pizza on Friday. I don't want pizza again. I'd rather have tacos."

"No tacos. The soft-shell tacos clog up my braces and the hard shells make my teeth hurt."

"Well the pizza gets stuck in your braces, too. Either way you look gross when you eat."

"Mom! He called me gross! I can't help it because I have braces."

"Don't call your brother gross."

I sigh heavily and try to think of a neutral place to dine.

"What about chicken? Chicken is soft and we haven't had it in two or three days."

"No way! That chicken taste like Grandma's pork chops. We're tired of pork chops."

I drive around aimlessly for another thirty minutes, but we cannot all agree on a restaurant. Finally, I tell the boys, "I'm going back home and since we have very little food in the cupboards and I am completely exhausted, I'll just have to make you a 'wish sandwich'. My mom made me one once.

Don't ask me what it is either. You'll see in a moment."

By the time they wash their hands, I have prepared their meal. They sit down and analyze the sandwich before them. There are two slices of bread with mustard in between. That's all.

"Mom, what's this? Where's the meat?"

"You've gotta wish for it."

They close their eyes and wish for meat. When they open their eyes, nothing has changed.

"Where's the meat?"

"Gee, the same thing happened to me when I was kid and boy, after that, I was really excited whenever there actually was some meat in my sandwich."

After a few bites, they ask, "Can we call Grandma to see is she has some of those pork chops left?"

Fashion Models

I'm from a big family tree filled with dynamic, big boned women who have large feet and broad, childbearing hips. I'm proud of these women. They're the keep-it-simple, easy on the eyes sort of divas. You know, those "You're taking too long; I'll do it myself," no nonsense females who aren't afraid to have a slice of cake after dinner. We're just as likely to start a trend as we are to follow one.

Consequently, I am not easily persuaded to purchase anything simply because it looks good on a 5'11", 105 pound cover girl. I figure that if it looks great on her, it's bound to look awful on me. I would love to be 6 feet tall, but unless there's some miracle of modern medicine looming on the horizon, I'm pretty much stuck at my present height of 5-5.

I haven't weighed 105 pounds since high school; I mean the ninth grade of high school. I could reach that weight again with a lot of exercise, celery, and misery but I'd still be short. Why bother? Actually, I like having some flesh between my bones and my skin. It's a good look for me.

I have nothing against models. Beauty is to be appreciated, not envied or despised. I don't have to hate "them" to love me. Fashion models provide a valuable service. What would the world be like without them? What would the rich and famous do with their time if they couldn't go to Milan and New York and pay a bunch of money to watch these women walk back and forth on a runway? I would go to their homes and model for them at a much cheaper price, but so far no one has asked me. I watch these fashion shows on television for free but I guess it's not the same as being there.

Without cover girls, there would be nothing to look at while waiting in the check out line at the grocery store but pictures of aliens and two-headed dogs. There would be nothing to read at the beauty salon if we didn't have fashion magazines. Doctor's waiting rooms would be filled with sports magazines and old copies of

"Popular Mechanics." Yuck.

I have several friends who are models. We get along just swell. In fact, I've been quite worried about the runway models. They are the ones that strut down those narrow platforms in Paris wearing a top designer's latest interesting, but totally impractical, $700 swim suits.

I'm worried about them for a couple of reasons. First of all, what are they so unhappy about? They frown. They glare. They have dark circles painted under their eyes. They make a gazillion dollars an hour and they're in Paris for goodness sakes! I know it's hard work but I promise you that if it were me, I'd be grinning so big, they'd have to wipe the lipstick off my earrings.

The other reason that I'm concerned about my leggy friends is an unconfirmed rumor that many models are being injured during the shows. This tragedy lends credibility to my theory that one's hair should not weigh more than one's body.

It seems that when these poor ladies reach the end of the runway and do that ever so cool turn-spin hair-flip thing; they tilt their heads too far to one side. It's hard to balance on those stilt like shoes, and the heavy weight of their hair just pulls them right off the stage! Broken bones. Humiliation. Terrible stuff.

Surely you've noticed that the high fashion set is wearing their hair shorter these days. That's the reason, believe it or not.

I don't mind riding the latest fashion horse if the styles and colors look good on me. Neon colors are big right now. I look ill when I wear lime green. I don't care who says it's chi chi. I'm not buying it.

I'm certainly not in a position to dictate fashion but let me just offer this observation. If the threads of the seams of the garment are not visible before you put the outfit on, they should not be visible after you put the outfit on. That's fabric's way of screaming, "This is too tight! Please get a larger size!"

Tight clothes can hinder your circulation and make your legs numb. Next thing you know, you topple over just like those models.

Fruitcake Party

I'm sure she meant well, but Grandma blew it big time. It was my first real birthday party. I had just turned 6 years old.

Mom had decorated the house with balloons and crepe paper. The paper plates, cups, and napkins all matched the festive tablecloth. All of my little friends came wearing their finest party attire. We pinned the tail on the donkey and played musical chairs. We were having so much fun until Grandma brought out the cake.

She volunteered to bake the cake for the party. I just knew that she'd make me a big, moist, yellow cake with chocolate icing. That's still my favorite. However, for reasons unknown, Grandma whipped up a big, moist fruitcake. Fruit cake with icing, for goodness sake! Six-year-olds do not like fruitcake. I was the laughingstock of the neighborhood. To this day, I dread birthday parties.

My children do not share my fear of crepe paper and fruitcake. They insist on having a birthday party every year and it is always such an ordeal. First, we have to decide on a place. Each year, they want something more exciting and expensive. Once we decide on a location, we make out the guest list. Left to their own devices, we would have every child in the city at the party.

"Son we have to narrow this listen down to 10 boys," I say upon receiving a three-page computer printout of names.

"But Mom, those are all my very best friends. I can't leave anyone out."

"Son, come on now, I don't even recognize half of these names. You've included everyone you know. I'm sorry but this is just too many people. Who is Jeremy anyway?"

"He's the fastest kid in third grade. He's gotta come."

"OK, who is Aziz?"

"He gave me one of his Twinkies at lunch. He's my friend."

"Is this Harold kid the one that I always see in the principal's office?"

"The teachers don't understand him, Mom. He's a good boy.

He doesn't even eat dirt anymore at recess since he started taking that medication."

Exasperated, I try a different approach.

"Son, let's start by making a list of all the kids that invited you to their birthday parties." I scan the list again looking for familiar names. "I don't see Kenneth's name. You just went to his party last week. What about him?'

"He called me a poophead. He's not my friend anymore."

"Well several of these other boys called you a poophead, too. I heard them. Should I cross their names out for you?"

We share a laugh and I give him the list.

"Darling, life is full of difficult choices. Give me 10 names. The others will understand. I'm sure their parents do the same thing."

He looks at me like I invented algebra and slithers off to his room sulking.

At the party, the boys bowl and then deposit a day's pay into the video games scattered throughout the room. Everyone seems to be having a good time. My son is almost gracious when he opens the gift box that contains a tie. He murmurs, "Thank you" and drops it on the ground with the wrapping paper.

Convinced that we've pulled off a successful party, I'm about to sit down and enjoy a slice of chocolate sheet cake when I notice that Harold hasn't touched his cake or ice cream.

"Harold, what's wrong?" I inquire.

"I wanted fruitcake," he replies.

You just can't win, can you?

Allergic to Baths

My darling sons are allergic to soap and water. It causes them to be clean which is a condition they find uncomfortable. Therefore, they avoid baths as much as possible.

When we lived up north, on the advice of their pediatrician, we only gave them baths every other night because their skin was always so dry. That was when they were toddlers. But they constantly remind us of their old bathing schedule as if it were one of the Ten Commandments.

I always tell them the same thing. "Raise both your arms. Now turn your head to the right and sniff, turn your head to the left and sniff." I don't ask them if they smell anything because they never do. Instead, I say, "You did not have that odor when you left home this morning with a clean body and clean clothing. Something happened today that changed all of that. It is my hope that you enjoyed whatever caused you to get that dirt under your nails, but fun has a price."

Their eyes glaze over, and I have to stop myself from going off into a long lecture about dancing to the music and paying the piper which really isn't relevant but I'm trying to cram so many lessons into 18 short years.

Anyway, I continue, "It is a congressional law that you take a bath or shower every day unless you're ill or very late for work. If you go to school tomorrow smelling like that, I can be arrested for teacher abuse."

If they even hear me. They certainly don't believe me, but they start walking toward their bedroom. I smile at their retreating backs because I had the same allergy when I was a child.

I went through the most elaborate ruse to make it appear that I had taken a bath. I ran the water until the tub almost overflowed. Then I tossed in a handful of dirt from the aloe vera plant in my room. I stuck one foot in the water and stomped around on the mat so it would be wet. I wet my towels and the soap. I even washed my face and neck because my folks always checked behind my ears like if it was clean there then surely the rest of me was dirt free. I could have bathed in half the time it took me to pretend to bathe. I only forgot one little thing.

I didn't lock the door.

Mom walked in and busted me big-time. I was sitting on the toilet with my hand in the bath water making these great splashing sounds. She was not pleased. Bathing in that cold, dirty water taught me a lesson I never forgot.

Kids don't have that kind of imagination anymore. Three minutes after I sent him off to scrub a dub dub, Junior came back with his pajamas on and said, "All clean."

I raised my right eyebrow as I surveyed his dirty hands and touched his arm. It was as dry as sandpaper.

"Son, did you really get in the tub?" I asked in a doubtful tone. He lowered his head, "No ma'am."

"You will bathe every morning and every night for two weeks starting tonight," I said in a voice loud enough to carry down the hall.

"Oh no!" he groaned.

"Oh yes," I said. "Malcolm! What are you doing in there?" I asked his brother.

"I'm getting super clean, Mom!" he yelled back.

Allergy cured. Don't you just love those old fashioned remedies?

Happy Camper

I am not a happy camper.

Specifically, I'm referring to that Jellystone Park, Yogi Bear, and Boo Boo kind of camping. Certainly, I can appreciate the esthetic beauty and sensory delights of a bed of soft pine needles beneath a canopy of dense, green leaves. I have seen brilliant sunlight filter through moist leaves and cast a miniature rainbow on the crystal clear puddles below.

It was cute.

I don't mind a long hike or a nature walk. I enjoy picnics by the lake. I just don't like to sleep outside. I went to school for 20 years so that I would not have to sleep outside or eat food cooked over an open fire. Roughing it for me is a diet soda and cheap toilet tissue.

I'm sharing this secret with you because my three men are bugging me about going camping. We already have a big tent. In the summer, we put it up in the backyard and they sleep in it. I stay in the house and sleep in the middle of the bed with my stuffed animals. What's wrong with that? We're pretty much together. I don't have a stiff back in the morning, and they can come inside to shower.

My family says that sleeping in the back yard is not really camping. They have a tent, sleeping bags, mosquitoes, stars, grass, flashlights, and they sleep in their clothes. That's camping to me.

I have encouraged them to go explore the great outdoors without me. I have been camping. When I was a child, my parents took me camping all the time. I hated it. Most of the time, I sat in the car and read Nancy Drew books.

Sometimes I would fish with them. I enjoy fishing but I will not touch worms, minnows, or fish. But if someone baits my hook, I will fish for hours. Camping is wonderful for people that like that sort of thing.

I am not one of them.

Every few months, it's something else with these guys. They want a dog. They want a swimming pool. They want home cooked meals. This camping phase will pass, too.

Yesterday, my youngest tax deduction started in on me again.

"Mom, can we go camping?" he asked for the hundredth time.

"Son, you can go camping with your dad and brother anytime. I don't like camping."

"But Mom, it's no fun if you don't go."

"I promise you. It will be more fun without me there. I don't want to go."

Incredibly, as if we'd never discussed this before, he asked me again, "Why not?"

"Son," I said, "just listen:

I've never ever liked to camp.
The air is cold. The ground is damp.
The birds are noisy in the trees.
The long, tall grass makes mommie sneeze.
I am afraid of wolves and bears.
I do not like them here or there.
I do not like them anywhere.
I'd much prefer to shop at Sam's.
Oh yes I would son, Mom-I-Am.

I do not like the feel of fish
Unless they're fried and on a dish.
I do not want to steal your joy.
Go with your dad or with the boys.
Oh yes, I know, "Matt's mom" is cool.
She touches frogs. She's good at pool.
Perhaps you should go camp with her
If that is what you would prefer.

I simply do not like to camp.
I'd rather lick a hundred stamps.
I would not like it here or there.
I would not like it anywhere.
My son, I do not like to camp.
Please understand me, Mom-I-AM.

He laughed and said, "Did Dr. Seuss eat green eggs and ham when he went camping? Let's have that when we go camping. Oh, Mommy, I can't wait to go camping."

I guess we're going camping.

Get The Phone

I can't believe it. I lost my job. Well, they called it a reassignment but really I got the old boot. After all these years, of loyal, dedicated service, I was dismissed without so much as a day's notice or a Timex watch. You know, you give your all to these people, day after day, year after year of faithful, efficient, prompt, all-American work ethic and what do you get for your trouble? More trouble, that's what.

Now I'm not talking about my regular 9-5. No, this was one of my little side gigs that I've had for over a decade. The pay wasn't very good but I enjoyed it and, actually, I was very good at it. I hardly ever got any complaints. It wasn't a highly skilled position, I suppose almost anyone could do it. But I still think my seniority should have been given some consideration.

But no, they went and replaced me with this young kid that hasn't even graduated from school yet. Can you believe that? If you even find a hair on his chin, I assure you that it just fell out of one of his bushy eyebrows. Yeah, I'll admit it. He's a little faster than I am but other than that, he's got nothing on me.

I'm so upset that I don't know what to do with myself. It was my job, darn it! I've always answered the telephone!

Now, my son is the official phone man.

Sometimes I think the boy has dog ears or something. He grabs that receiver before the "ing" leaves the ring. I keep telling him that it has to ring twice before the caller ID is activated. Not that we screen our calls or anything. Well, OK, yeah, we screen our calls sometimes. You've just got to be in the right mood to talk to some people you know. Anyway, he's so quick on the draw that you'd think Shaquille O'Neal or one of those Victoria's Secret women was going to call here at any minute.

But if it's not for him, Heaven help the person on the other end.

He lays the receiver on the counter and says, "Mom!" or "Dad!" and then he goes back to playing video games.

If we heard him, fine, if not, oh well.

Sometimes, I walk past the receiver and it's lying on the floor making that awful "dun, dun" sound like a big truck backing up.

I stand in front of him until he notices me and say, "Did someone call? Who was on the phone?"

"Oh yeah," he says. "Some lady wanted to talk to you. Didn't you hear me call you? That was a long time ago."

"No, I didn't hear you. What was the lady's name?"

"Sue? I think. Maybe it was Sharon. Something with an 'S' in it."

I run to the caller ID. Nothing. And I'm not a star-69 kind of person. There's something about calling someone's home and saying, "Did you call me?" that intimidates me. I did it once and the person said, "No, who are you?" So I hung up and the stranger called me back and said, "Did you just call me?" It was awful. We went back and forth like that several times until I finally recognized the voice and said, "Mama, is that you?"

And it gets worse. On the rare occasion that he writes a message down, he forgets to give it to me. Usually, I find a scrap of paper on the floor two days later that says, "Sue or Sharon called. It's real important."

So Sue and/or Sharon, forget leaving messages with the kid.

Until I can figure out a way to get my position back, if it's important, just call me at work.

He Dressed Himself

He was young. The kind of young that thinks a 20-year-old is ancient history. He had seen just enough through those big green eyes to acquire a hint of wariness that caused him to cling to the hem of his mother's dress like a small piece of lint. Yet, his innocent, easy smile and fluid gestures indicated that his trust could be bought with a small candy bar or a big puppy.

His mother and older sister wore their understated affluence across their proud shoulders and down their slender, well-tanned frames. Chanel, Donna Karan for Kids, Halston, Movado. I took this designers inventory out of appreciation and curiosity. The ladies looked so nice, but the little boy, well, he looked–um, shall we say, colorful? Very colorful.

Little Skippy was wearing pinstriped pants, red and blue. They were about an inch shy of covering his ankles and the green socks that he wore. His short-sleeved shirt was covered with stars and moons; green stars and yellow moons. Skippy's hair was combed in four directions, none of which seemed to be the natural pattern of growth. A thin, brown belt held his ensemble together.

I was behind Skippy and his family in a long line at the convenience store. The little boy stared at me until I smiled at him. Suddenly shy, he giggled and turned away. Sensing potential danger, I suppose, his mother glanced back and his sister did a graceful pirouette in my direction. Having satisfied herself that I was a mild-mannered housewife on a mission to buy toilet tissue, his mother smiled. His sister then borrowed her mother's smile and shared it with me as well.

"You have lovely children," I said.

"Thank you," she replied. Then she quickly added as if in apology, "My son dressed himself."

Skippy looked at his mom and then at me, awaiting my reaction.

"You're kidding," I exclaimed. I looked down at Skippy. "You did a good job Skippy. You're a big boy. I think you look great."

Skippy beamed. His sister rolled her eyes in disbelief. Skippy took a step toward me and said, "You know what? These are my favorite pants. When grandpa was in the big box, they put a flag on it and it was just like my pants. My grandma got the flag, but she's gonna give it to me someday. She promised."

"Well, I'm sure she will if she promised," I said.

Encouraged, Skippy continued, "And my shirt is for my daddy. He flies air-o-planes way up in the stars. I'm gonna be a air-o-plane pilot just like my daddy someday. Then I can fly to visit my grandpa way up in the sky."

With tears in her eyes, Skippy's mother said, "Darling, is that why you chose those clothes? I didn't know that. You really miss grandpa don't you?"

Skippy nodded. His mother turned to me and said, "My father recently passed away."

I offered condolences as she paid for their purchases. They started to leave, and then Skippy ran back and gave me a great big hug.

Back in my car, I noticed the chocolate stain on my blouse. That's a small price to pay for wisdom.

Thanks, Skippy. You really are a big boy.

He Just Walks Away

I have searched the depths of my soul, evaluated all of my motivations, and consulted my closest and wisest friends and I truly believe that what I'm about to say is not male-bashing.

I am simply making an observation about a particular behavior that I have observed in my husband, who is a good man. My friends tell me that they, too, have seen this conduct in their male counterparts. Therefore, I am simply wondering aloud about something I find puzzling and, actually, quite annoying. And if in the long run it does prove to be male-bashing, well, I'm sorry.

Here's a typical scenario. The love of my life and I are in the kitchen engaged in what I believe is a conversation. Granted, he's not saying much and he looks bored but still we're spending quality time together. I might be telling him about a conversation that occurred while I was having lunch with a friend or something that I read in a magazine when suddenly he just walks away! Right in the middle of a sentence he just wanders off as if I'm not even there. I know I'm talking because my mouth is moving and sounds are coming out of it. He doesn't even wait until I pause for breath or reach a period. Right between syllables, he turns his back and heads for the door.

He wouldn't be that rude to a perfect stranger. I know because I've seen him spend hours talking to the most boring person in the room at some of the best parties we've ever been too. Afterwards he says, "Why didn't you rescue me? That guy spent two hours telling me about his job as a paper clip inspector. I couldn't get away from him. Didn't you see me give you the signal?"

Like most married couples, we have several nonverbal ways of communicating distress. When his eyes roll back in his head until only the whites show, that means "Help! I feel like the bailiff at OJ's trial!"

Sure, I saw the signal but the fellow he was with saw it too. He thought my husband was choking on his mini quiche and did the

Heimlich maneuver on my sweetie. Frankly, I was laughing too hard to help him.

Anyway, I said, "I have told you a million times how to get away from those people and you insist on sinking with the ship. Just stick out your hand and say, 'It's really nice to meet you. Please excuse me, my stomach is a little upset. I need to find the restroom." Then just politely walk away.

He will talk to anyone, at length, about nothing. So why does he find it so easy to ignore me when I'm talking?

He says that I do the same thing in my own way with him and the kids. According to them, I merely pretend to listen even though my mind is a million miles away. This is totally untrue. I listen to every word and I have good eye contact.

To this, Mr. Manners responds, "Yesterday, I told you that your hair was on fire and I'd just eaten Tide. You nodded and said, 'OK dear, that's fine. I'll pick up the kids after school."

"You just talk too low. I thought you said that you had a flat tire and the kids needed a ride."

So I'm not perfect but I still want him to listen to me for hours with a sweet smile and adoring eyes like he did when we were dating or at least say, "Are you finished?"

Clearly, I'm just wasting my time nagging him about his breech of etiquette. Yesterday, in the middle of my story about Shelly's ingrown toenail, he stuck out his hand and said, "It's really nice to meet you—"

Can't Sleep A Wink

Sshhh!!! Did you hear that?

Wait. See, there it goes again.

I'm more certain now than ever that this house is possessed. It moans and groans as things go bump in the night. The stairs creek and the windows hiss like snakes. Something is in the attic dragging its heavy feet across the rafters; slowly it paces, to then fro.

My husband doesn't believe me. He never hears anything but the wind howling at the door, but I have an explanation for that.

The Thing doesn't stir when he's home. It only happens when he's away. Really.

My husband says, "All houses make noises. Most of that noise is coming from the heater or the refrigerator, and the rest is just your overactive imagination."

"No it is not." I insist. "Heaters don't go 'oooh, oooh, oooh' like Streisand with a respiratory infection or 'Hey, girlie, I'm gonna get you,' now do they?"

"Honey, come on now. You heard something say, 'Hey, girlie, I'm gonna get you'? I told you not to take that cold medicine before you go to bed."

"Well, that's what I heard. I was in the bathroom brushing my teeth and I saw a big shadow by the window and that's when it talked to me."

"Dear, there's a tree by that window. It probably brushed against the glass and made some kind of sound. I'll trim the branches tomorrow."

"It was not the tree! It had three arms and a top hat. I know a monster when I see one!"

It's odd to find myself in this place. There was a time at the beginning of our marriage when I had trouble sleeping because my husband was in bed with me. No, let me explain that a little more. See, after 20-something years of sleeping solo, to suddenly find that you have to share mattress space with another human being takes some getting used to. He snored. He insisted that I unwind the sheet from around my body like a cocoon so that he could have some cover too. Every time he turned over, the mattress moved and I woke up. Plus, there was all of that heat!

For the first few nights, we were all cuddled up and cozy until finally I said, "Would you mind moving back to your side. I can't sleep like this; it's too hot and you're lying on my hair."

He quickly moved over and said, "Thank goodness! I haven't gotten a good night's sleep all week. I thought women liked that snuggling stuff. Man, my arm is numb, and my legs keep cramping up. Now I can stretch out and relax."

"You don't have to get that happy about it."

"Aw baby, I love having you next to me but you know, just not right next to me when I'm trying to sleep, that's all. Oh, and by the way, you need to lay off those refried beans for a while. Not that I'm complaining, but they don't seem to agree with your stomach."

As time went by, I found comfort in his presence just an arm's length away. When he's gone, the bed feels uncomfortable, my feet get cold and that stupid monster starts running through the house.

Last week, my son even heard it. He came flying into my bedroom in the middle of the night.

"Mom, did you hear that! Somebody was singing. It sounded like that lady on your CD."

"Streisand. I know. I heard it. Come on. You can sleep in here. That's daddy's picture on the pillow. The monster is afraid of daddy.

" Now good night."

I Hate Shopping

Believe it or not, there are a lot of women like me who really detest going shopping. There are also many men who enjoy the mall. Personally, I only know one of them but I've read about the others and I'm sure that they exist.

I can't single out just one thing that I dislike about shopping. Actually, it's a number of little things that add up to a totally unpleasant experience. For instance, I don't like all the walking. The floors are hard and the aisles are crowded. I went into one store looking for a simple white blouse. They had women's blouses on three different floors. Why? I ask you. Put all the blouses together and make my life less complicated, why don't you?

I had to find the escalator and trudge from floor to floor three times just to find a white blouse in my size that appeared to have been designed for a modest adult, and didn't cost an arm and a leg. Why can't we have one women's department anymore? Why does the price of the clothes escalate as the floors go higher? I would think that they would put the clothes for wealthy women on the lowest floor so that all that walking wouldn't inconvenience them.

Anyway, the men have all of their stuff conveniently located in one section of the department store. They've got suits, ties, shoes, and socks all right there together and usually near an exit. They don't have to walk all over the store carrying a pair of pants trying to find a matching sweater. Someone must have requested that the ladies have seven different sections of dresses but it sure wasn't me.

My shopaholic friends will drag me all over town to save $2 on a belt. We use up $10 worth of gas to save two bucks! They even dare suggest going to the Galleria to find a good deal. There are no bargains in the Galleria. Galleria is Latin for "if you must look at the price tag before you look at the size, you can't afford it."

Which reminds me, I totally do not understand this concept of saving money as promoted by retailers. How can you spend money and save money at the same time? It doesn't matter if it's marked down 90 percent. If I had to pay something for it, I did not save any money. Saving, by definition, means to avoid spending. Let's just call it what it is ~ a better value. You simply cannot buy two and save. Of course, I fall for it and buy two anyway but I do know better. That's our uniquely American economics at work.

I'm trying to teach our kiddos this concept of restraint and budgeting. They are not grasping it at all. Last week, we pulled into the parking lot of a megastore. As we walked the half-mile to the entrance, I gave them lecture No. 53 for the hundredth time.

"Boys, don't get in here and start asking me for toys and CDs. I came here to get a broom and that is that we're buying today. Dad and I are not made out of money and we cannot afford to buy everything that you see on television. So just don't ask for a thing today because the answer is 'no.'"

As soon as we cleared the automatic doors, they ran off to the electronics department to play video games. While searching for the perfect broom, I bumped into an old friend from high school. While we were chatting my youngest son walked up clutching a hideous $5 T-shirt with some mutant alien on the front of it.

"Mom," he pleaded, "I know we're poor but will you please buy me this T-shirt? I have some money in my piggy bank at home and I promise I'll pay you back. All of my friends have a shirt like this. Please Mom, can I? Please, please?"

Visions of our next class reunion passed through my head at warp speed. I would be the laughingstock of our entire class. They would all shake their heads and whisper as I walked by. My poor child had no idea that I wanted to disown him at that very moment.

"Sweetie, of course you can get a T-shirt. If you see another one that you like, get it, too. Find your brother and tell him to meet us by the riding lawnmowers. I think dad said he wanted a green one."

No, I'm not proud of myself, but I must say that my husband was thrilled when my son whispered to him that he would probably get a riding mower for his birthday.

More shopping.

Yuck.

I Forgot

My grandmother was fond of saying, "I've forgotten more than you'll ever know". At the time, I thought she was tripping. (That's Ebonics for "losing her marbles.") It seemed like such a silly excuse for her inability to remember my birthday. After all, there were only 61 other grandchildren in the family!

Well, I'm not laughing anymore. At the tender age of thirty-something, not only have I forgotten my children's birth dates but sometimes I can't even get their names straight. I can't remember the directions to places I've visited dozens of times. I misplace my car keys at least once a week. I can't remember my husband's shirt size.

It's $17^1/_2$ or 18 inches, I think. His neck is too big, anyway.

It's very frustrating to keep forgetting these simple things all the time. The tooth fairy and I finally decided that it was easier for her just to leave the kids' money in my wallet.

My best friend says that I have a yuppie condition known as "sometimers," as in "sometimes I remember things and sometimes I don't."

Right now I can't remember what I had for breakfast. I know that coffee was involved because coffee is my life force. I just don't recall whether I consumed food while I drank it. It was certainly not memorable food.

My boys get so exasperated with me because I always exit through the wrong door at the mall. The malls simply have too many doors. Then, I have to allow an extra half-hour in my schedule for locating my vehicle after shopping. I suppose you would tell me to just write everything down. I tried that, but then I could never find my notes.

I have tried to explain my problem to my high-tech offspring.

"Listen," I said, "everyone's mind is like a wonderful computer. Now, Mommy has a fabulous hard drive. It's at least six gigabytes. However, my Ram is not very good. I only have 512 kilobytes."

They nodded in immediate comprehension, but my computer-illiterate spouse was still exasperated. With my grandest smile, the one in which both dimples show, I said: "Love of my life, when it comes to long-term memory, for things like your name and our address, I've got a binder full of paper. But for short-term memory, like the names of people we meet at parties, I've only got a 3-by-5 index card."

The truth is that I've established that I can only remember four new names at a time. That's why our dining table seats six. If I get a fifth name in my head, one of those other names is automatically deleted. At receptions, I spend the entire evening talking to the same four people because I can't recall anyone else's name.

I went to see a therapist about my condition, but he wasn't helpful at all. I sat on a hard couch with too many pillows and told him about my awful problem. He said, "What have you forgotten recently?"

"Well, I forgot my purse today," I said.

He raised his brows and said, "Really? What does your purse mean to you?"

I hate stupid questions like that. It's just a brown purse. It was a gift, but I don't remember who gave it to me. It doesn't really mean anything to me.

"Of course it does," he said. "What do you carry in your purse?"

I had to think a moment. I usually carry a few pictures, an ATM card, my checks, some cash and a couple of credit cards. At that, he abruptly stood up and exclaimed: "Oh my, look at the time! Our session must conclude, Mrs. Anderson. When you come back next week, remember to bring your purse."

Then he flew out of the room like a leaf in a hurricane.

Of course, I didn't go back. I couldn't remember where his office was located.

And you know, the more I think about it, I do believe it was actually my aunt who used to say, "I've forgotten more than you'll ever know."

In Search of Peace

The horror I felt upon reading about the deadly terrorist bomb-ings that took place in Kenya and Tanzania is indescribable.

The following Saturday morning, I opened my newspaper to a gruesome photo depicting an eerie collage of bodies, buildings and blood. Tears of sorrow hindered my efforts to read the eyewitness accounts of the fatal blasts.

As of this moment, the world is not sure who is responsible or why the perpetrators thought that this act of evil would bring peace to their turmoil. During troublesome moments like these, I with-draw to a place deep inside myself and ponder the unknown vari-ables of life.

This time, in a flight of pure fancy, I climbed aboard an imagi-nary aircraft and set out on a voyage in search of Peace. Perhaps if I could find Peace, I could persuade it to settle down and dwell among us for more than a fortnight. Surely, that photo alone, those mangled torsos, the silent screams, would persuade Peace to be still.

We left New York cruising at a low altitude over the choppy waters of the Atlantic until we arrived at our first stop, historic Northern Ireland. I saw Protestants, Catholics, and fresh graves, but Peace was no where to be found. So we jetted over France, passed Italy, and crossed the Adriatic Sea before we landed again, this time in the former Yugoslavia. Bullet casings littered the streets filled with hundreds of thousands of homeless civilians. There were rumors of a Serbian crackdown on Albanian separatists but there was no sign of Peace.

Still hopeful, our optimistic pilot cruised south past the fighting in Turkey and Syria, to the country of Iraq. We asked the United Nations Arms Inspectors if they had found Peace hiding out some-where during their searches. "No," they said. "If Peace had been here, the sanctions wouldn't have been necessary."

Distressed, we refueled and looked eastward. We flew over Iran to Afghanistan, which looked hopeful from a distance. Up close, however, we discovered that years of civil war had brought too much sorrow for Peace to remain in that place.

Further we traveled, to China then Russia, in search of satisfaction. We tasted salty tears in the Pechora River. I smelled poverty and heard politics but, alas, again, no Peace.

Across the Pacific Ocean, in record time, we landed in a drug-infested area of South America where artificial Peace grew tall in a field of dreams.

"Let's go to Mexico," I said to the pilot. "If we don't find Peace there, take me home."

Colorful villas and beautiful beaches welcomed me to Mexico. Surely, Peace is here, I thought. However, when I ventured away from the resorts and the lavish lifestyles of the upper class, I found many desperate, impoverished people clamoring for a ride back to the States with me.

"Peace is in America," they said.

Peace is in America! I went all over the world looking for Peace and I could have found it right at home. Quickly, we rushed to the West Coast ~ no Peace; over to the East Coast ~ no Peace; along the Bible Belt where the hate groups chased me away ~ no Peace.

Back home, alone in my room, I hung my head in defeat. Then, a small voice whispered to me, "Here I am. I'm the one you're looking for. I am Peace. I was with you all the time.

"Peace is not an object that you can find. Peace is an ideal that you must create. When there is peace inside of all of you, there will be peace outside of all of you."

"Peace," I said, "that's too much for even me to imagine."

Jack & Jill

On the whole, I like nursery rhymes. Children learn important skills from memorizing and reciting nursery rhymes; they learn vocabulary words, rhyme and rhythm.

They can also learn morals and values while being entertained.

When my boys were toddlers, I spent hours reading fairy tales and nursery rhymes to them as they sat in my lap or rocked in their cradle.

However, because I've never been a slave to tradition, I never hesitated to change the verses to a nursery rhyme if I felt it conflicted with our family values. I didn't know anything about political correctness then; it just seemed to me that there was something wrong with "Jack and Jill went up the hill, To fetch a pail of water; Jack fell down, and broke his crown, And Jill came tumbling after."

I just couldn't tell it to them that way.

I don't know why Jack fell, perhaps he stumbled or encountered a slippery slope. It's really not important why he fell because we all fall sometimes. He fell so hard that he "broke his crown." I believe that means he got a concussion. His head probably hit a rock because quarterbacks like Steve Young and Troy Aikman always get concussions when their heads hit that hard turf, but I don't think that happens much when a fellow just falls on some grass.

Anyway, after Jack fell, Jill came tumbling after him. More problems.

First of all, they should consider finding another well that's not so difficult to reach. This one must be on a very steep hill since Jill not only fell but also she rolled end over end after she fell. Maybe it was a coincidence that they both slipped, but I always got the feeling that Jill fell down just because Jack did. My husband says they were probably holding hands, but they should have been carrying some pails for that water. I guess we'll never know what really happened on that fateful day long ago.

My version of the story caused my oldest boy some problems

during those first few weeks of preschool. When called on by his teacher to recite "Jack and Jill", my 4-year-old said.

"Jack and Jill went up the hill to fetch a pail of water. Jack fell down and hurt his head so Jill, who was a medical doctor, stopped the bleeding with the sleeve from her blouse and then she picked Jack up and helped him back down the hill.

While Jack rested, Jill went back and got the water so that she could make Jack some soup."

My son didn't get called on much after that.

I never even told the boys the second stanza of that rhyme. "Then up Jack got and off did trot, As fast as he could caper, To old Dame Dob, who patched his nob, With vinegar and brown paper."

What happened to Jill? Did he just leave her behind? Good grief.

This poem is all about relationship problems. Jill was too co-dependent and Jack was overwhelmed with too much responsibility (get the water, drag the old lady up the hill–). I bet Jack just snapped and had a breakdown.

That's too bad. They seemed like such a nice couple.

Oh well.

Type A Mom

In retrospect, I guess we knew early on that there was something a little different about me. You know, strange in a "I hope she grows out of it" sort of way.

The first time it popped up, I was only nine-years-old. My mother came home from work and found me lying across my bed bawling like a colicky infant before you figure out it's not colic at all but the kid is allergic to cheap formula.

She rushed to my side and asked, "What's wrong pumpkin? Are you sick?"

I could barely hiccup out the words, "Something terrible happened at school today."

"Did you get expelled? Did someone hurt you? Did that real short girl take your lunch money again?"

"No, it was worse than that," I mumbled into my tear-stained pillow.

"Well what is it? I can't help you if you don't tell me what happened."

"I, I, I made a "B" on my math test Mom. My life is over."

To her credit, my mother didn't laugh in my face but she should have. Yes, I'm a classic Type A personality. "A" for assertive, ambitious, and always achieving. I have no idea how to do nothing. I can copy other people doing nothing but I have no original nothingness to offer.

I try to do nothing but then I pass something that needs to be done, and I forget to not do it. And I'm not alone. There are many of us. We would all work ourselves into an early grave if nature hadn't devised a simple plan to keep us from self-destructing.

Type A parents have Type C children. C stands for "couldn't care less" about anything that isn't fun. That would include most things that we parents care deeply about.

"Son," I ask, "why would you wait until Sunday night to tell me that you need 100 Popsicle sticks and some liquid cement to build a fort for a project that's due tomorrow?"

"I forgot," he replies nonchalantly.

"But you reminded me 10 times that two weeks ago I promised to take you and your friends to the movies this weekend. Why didn't you forget that too?"

"I don't know. That's weird, huh? So are we going to the store or what?"

On his last math test he made a 50! When I saw the test score, I got chest pains and my nose started bleeding.

"Be cool Mom," he said. "Everybody got a low score except that nerdy girl Tammy and she cries whenever she makes a 'B'. She even let some short kid take her lunch away from her today. What a loser."

I try to talk to him about "blazing paths where highways never ran" and he says, "Is that anything like cutting the grass? I hate to mow. I think I'm allergic."

I know he's my child. I watched him be born, and I was quite lucid because they wouldn't give me any of the drugs that I requested. He looks so much like me but he acts so unlike me.

He's added years onto my life.

All too often, I come home after a long, hard day, foaming at the mouth because bikes are in the driveway, mud is on the kitchen floor and dirty breakfast dishes are still in the sink.

My little guy just smiles at me and gives me an awesome hug. He pulls me by the hand and says, "Mom, come play with me. We can do that stuff later."

You know, maybe "C" stands for celestial. He's heaven's special gift to me.

Junk Food Junkie

The love of a parent knows no boundaries. A parent will beg the court for mercy on behalf of their unrepentant, ruthless son. A father will work three jobs to pay for his daughter's college education. A mother will dart in front of a moving vehicle to shield her baby from harm.

On the other hand, some animals actually eat their young. I don't condone this behavior, but I do understand it. Therefore, I will limit this discussion to human parents and their infinite love.

You see, I am determined to help my son kick his very destructive habit no matter what it costs me. We'll do a 12-step program, participate in group therapy, or even send him to military school if that is what it takes. We will find a cure for him and we won't give up until we do.

Unfortunately, my boy is a junk food junkie. If it has sugar in it, he'll eat it, and he'll eat it until it is all gone. It's gotten so bad that we have to lock up the Ho Hos. One night we found him in the kitchen eating the crumbs out of the cookie jar with his eyes closed. He was sleepwalking! The next day he didn't remember a thing.

I have tried to reason with Junior about his bad habit. "Son, it's not healthy to eat sweets all the time," I say. "Eventually you'll ruin your health and your teeth. Because of all this junk food, you don't have an appetite for nutritious food and you're gaining weight. This has got to stop."

"I can't help it," he replies. "I've tried to stop but my friends keep giving me candy. And plus, there's the voice–"

"What voice?"

"The cookie man. He lives in the cookie jar and every time I walk by he calls me, 'Junior! Junior! Please have a cookie. It's too crowded in here. I can't breathe. You've got to help me."

"Son, I thought I told you to stop bouncing that soccer ball on your head. Besides, that doesn't explain why you always eat the last two or three cookies."

"Oh, I eat those because the cookie man says that they're lonely."

There are times in the life of a parent when you just shake your head and walk away. This was one of those times.

So we just started hiding the cookies, foregoing the ice cream, drinking more water and basically doing whatever we could to starve that monkey off his back. Consequently, everyone suffered but it was well worth it especially when I found only one candy wrapper in his wastebasket at the end of the week.

"Junior, I'm proud of you. You've cut down on the candy. Normally, your trashcan is half full of wrappers. I only found one in there this week."

"Oh yeah. I didn't mean to put that in there. I've been stuffing them in my backpack and throwing them away at school. That's a good idea, huh? Then there's less trash to take out. So can I have a Ho Ho from the safe?"

There are times in the life of a parent when you just shake your head and walk away.

Grandpa the Baby Sitter

Contrary to what we've led our children to believe, there are a number of things that parents fear. There's the letter from the IRS that contains anything but a check. The personal phone call from your physician after a physical examination. A flat tire on a deserted road at night and, well, telephone conversations like this:

"Hi sweetie. It's Mom," I say when my youngest son answers the phone.

"Hi Mom! Where are you? Are you coming to get us?" The excitement in his voice gladdens my heart.

"No honey. We'll be home tomorrow, on Sunday. Remember? I said we would be back in two days."

"Friday and Saturday. That's two days," he rationalizes.

"Okay, 48 hours. I meant 48 hours." Kids take everything so literally.

"So you'll be home in 24 hours right?" Clearly, he'll do well in math next year.

"Actually, we'll be home in 27 hours."

"But you said–"

"Sweetie, we'll be home tomorrow. I promise. We'll be home in time for dinner."

I wink at my husband on the other side of the restaurant. He's irritated. He didn't want me to call home so soon.

"Are you being a good boy?"

"I sure am! I ate a spoonful of peas for Grandpa last night so he let me have cake for breakfast."

The first mommy alarm goes off in my head.

"Son, did you have anything else with the cake?"

"Um hmm. Cold pizza and milk."

 Calcium and tomatoes. There's some nutrition there I think.

"Caleb, when we left yesterday, you were wearing blue shorts and a white T-shirt. What are you wearing today?"

"Blue shorts and a purple and white T-shirt," he answers proudly.

"What purple and white T-shirt? I didn't pack a purple and white T-shirt."

"Well, it was white before I spilled grape juice on it. Grandpa said it was a waste of time to wash it 'cause grape juice don't never come out no way."

I must find a safe subject to discuss. I'm up to two mommie alarms now.

"Did you remember to brush your teeth before you went to bed?"

"Yep. Calvin said that if we brushed for 10 minutes, we wouldn't have to do it again this morning."

"Where is Calvin?" In the background, I hear loud voices and screaming.

"He's watching wrestling with Grandpa. You know that show you won't let us watch? It's really good."

I remind myself not to tell this child any national security secrets.

"Hey Mom, where are our gym bags anyway?"

"They're probably by the front door where your father left them. How did you brush your teeth without a toothbrush?"

"Oh, I found one in Grandpa's toolbox. And guess what Mom? We're going fishing when it gets dark and Grandpa says I can shine the flashlight in the water and make the fish come. We may even sleep on the boat if it stops raining."

We are now at a three-alarm alert and my husband is really frowning at me. "Where's your grandmother, Caleb?"

"She called a while ago. The church bus broke down in Arkansas so she won't be back until tomorrow. Uh-oh, Mom gotta go! Killer Karl is gonna strangle Mr. Wonderful with a crow bar. See ya!"

The line goes dead. I weigh my options as I slowly walk back to the table where my food is getting cold. Between bites of teriyaki chicken, my husband asks, "How are the kids?"

I douse the fretful fire with a cold beverage and reply like a working mother on a much-needed vacation.

"Great, they're having a ball."

Magoo & Dudley

Magoo and Dudley are such an odd pair. They are the best of friends, yet they seem to have nothing at all in common. They live together in the exclusive neighborhood of Lakeway a few miles outside of Austin, Texas.

Dudley is so big that he intimidates you at first meeting. He's quiet though and really quite harmless. He's quite advanced in years but he still does a mean cha-cha. His favorite pastime is sunning himself by the gorgeous, blue diving pool that overlooks Lake Travis. I think he'd just lie there all day if he could.

Magoo, on the other hand, is young and energetic. He's like a noisy toy that won't turn off until you remove the battery and tell your kid, "Sweetie, I don't know why the siren won't come on. I guess it's broken." Magoo is all over the place making sure everything is in order. He seems to be preparing for unexpected guests all day long. He takes some getting used to. All that yakking and smiling and buzzing about. You want to just tell him, "Buddy sit down and take a load off. Doesn't your face hurt from all that smiling and talking?"

I didn't say that, however, because I was a guest in their home and, anyway, that would be a stupid thing to say to a dog. At least, I think they're dogs. Their owners, Scott and Karen, don't think of them as dogs. To them, they're family.

Dudley is like an old uncle that retired from the military and just doesn't have a push-up left in him. He's a teenager, which is near the end of the road for a canine.

Magoo is like their little boy who thinks every day is his birthday. He's only a few years old and boy can he go! I'd tell you what kind of dogs they are if I knew. I'm not really a dog person. I like them now but I had a morbid fear of them for years because one used to chase me home from school every day for the entire nine months of third grade.

Anyway, Dudley is a huge, golden dog with a humongous head and big, droopy jowls. His ears and tail are short if that helps any.

I know you dog people are dying but I'm sorry. Magoo is a terrier though, I think. He's little and black and white with a longer tail.

Scott and Karen love those dogs in a way no one can measure. It's a special relationship.

So the story goes that a bunch of us spent the weekend at Scott and Karen's house, and this fellow Tim got the great idea to take Dudley for a walk. Scott said, "Don't walk him too far. He's kind of old." A short while later, Tim came running into the house to tell us that Dudley had collapsed by the side of the road. Scott flew out of that house at a speed that would put track star Michael Johnson to shame. Karen called the vet, and the rest of us just stood around helplessly.

Scott returned with Dudley in the back of his Jeep. He looked terrible. He was panting and his eyes were real red. Dudley was in pretty bad shape, too. Tim looked like John Wilkes Booth, and no one said a word to him. We gave Dudley water and put cool, wet towels on him.

Meanwhile, Magoo came running out of the house, took one look at Dudley and jumped into the driver's seat. He started barking and trying to turn the steering wheel as if to say, "What is wrong with you people? We've got to get my friend to the doctor right away! Quit wasting time and give me the keys!"

Fortunately, Scott's patience paid off and Dudley revived a short time later. He got out of the truck and went to lie down by the pool. All was well. Everyone was happy.

For a moment there, I was actually pretty frantic about that dog. I suppose it could be because I knew how sad my friends would be if something happened to their pet. Or it could be that I'm learning to love all of God's creatures, even the ones that lick my hands.

Meeting Her Parents

Americans don't generally practice arranged marriages; that is unless you count the occasional shotgun wedding, which in Texas we just call "real short engagements."

Generally speaking, however, we prefer the kiss-the-frog method of selecting a mate. You know, you date a lot of incompatible people until you find someone that you like so much you can actually break your mother's heart by telling her, "I won't be home for Christmas this year." That, my friend, is as good as saying "I do." At the very least, it's a strong "I might - if your family isn't totally weird."

Yes, it's important to know about your sweetheart's family before you make any arrangements whatsoever. I encourage young people to make an effort to meet their new love's family real early in the relationship, preferably even before the first date. I tell you it can save you a whole heap of trouble later on.

For example, years ago I once went over to a nice fellow's home and discovered his entire family sitting in the den watching television. I wondered what they were watching because they were all laughing and enjoying themselves immensely. It seemed like a nice domestic scene until I noticed that the television set wasn't turned on. In fact, there wasn't even a screen or a tube in the thing. When my date's brother took a pair of pliers and changed the station, I sort of knew that our relationship was doomed.

Then his mother said, "Bubba, why don't you adjust the antennae a bit and see if you can make them fuzzy lines disappear."

Bubba, my date, complied but he couldn't seem to get it quite right. He finally started to walk away from the set but his father said, "Freeze boy! That's it. It's perfect now."

Bubba had to stand there for an hour while his family watched whatever it was they were seeing on the TV. I would have left but I couldn't get his stupid dog off my leg.

Of course, I had a few dating faux pas at my home, too. I'll never forget the first time my future husband came over to meet my parents. My mother spotted him first and said, "Well, hello Bubba, it's good to see you again."

"Hello ma'am," he said. "My name is Alfred and we've never met before but it's very nice to meet you."

"Mama!" I hissed through clenched teeth, "Don't you remember? Poor Bubba died a year ago."

I was winking my right eye furiously trying to give her a clue. She was going to ruin everything. I might have to call Bubba again if this new guy didn't work out.

"Bubba died? But he was just over here last week, wasn't he?"

She had the gall to look distraught. She didn't even like Bubba or his dog. Then she noticed that my eyes had rolled back in my head, obviously seeking refuge from the humiliation.

"What's wrong pumpkin?" she inquired. "You seem to have a twitch in your right eye. Maybe you need glasses. You did walk right into that door this morning."

"No, Mama, I don't need glasses. And don't you have something to do?"

"Actually no. Let's take Allen into the backyard to meet your father."

"It's Alfred ma'am."

"Whatever."

My dad was in the back yard shooting cans with his rifle. He stopped, looked Alfred over and said, "Boy, did you hear about Bubba?"

"Yessir."

"Then you'll make sure she's home by eleven won't you?"

"Yessir!"

I was home at 9 o'clock.

Amazingly, a few years later, Alfred married me anyway which just goes to prove that love is as blind and crazy as Bubba's family. Bubba's married too, by the way. He had a real short engagement, but he's quite happy now.

Defective Kids

The same doctor delivered both of my children. She examined them thoroughly and assured us that they were perfectly healthy. On the day following each delivery, the pediatrician came by and looked the boys over. He performed various tests and then he, too, assured us that both of the kids were as fit as a fiddle.

We never missed a well-baby check-up. They went through the developmental stages right on schedule. We rocked them, read to them, and gave them vitamins every day. All of that and they still ended up with defects.

The oldest child, Junior, the one that screamed and woke us up at 2 AM every night for the first year of his life, has a speech problem. All he can say is, "Hm-m" and "It was OK."

My youngest, Ivan, has trouble seeing or hearing anything that isn't animated. And neither one of them can remember more than two things at a time.

Recently, Junior went to a sleepover birthday party at his best friend's home. When I picked him up, he was wearing the same clothes that he had worn the previous day. I always pack him a nice pair of pajamas and a change of clothes. He never uses them but it makes me feel like a good parent to provide them.

"How was the party son?" I asked as we left his friend's house.

"It was OK," he replied nonchalantly.

"Mrs. Smith said that you guys had fun playing Laser Tag. Did you score a lot of points?"

"Uh-hmm."

"How was the birthday cake? Was it the kind that you like with the creamy frosting?"

"It was OK," he said and immediately fell asleep. I hoped that it was the three hours of sleep and not boredom with my conversation that brought the sandman to our car so abruptly.

Back at home, I ask Ivan to hang up his coat, take out the trash, and make a pitcher of tea for lunch. Ten minutes later, he's sitting on the floor in front of the television still wearing his coat.

"Ivan!" I yell over the noise of the Rugrats, "What did I tell you to do?"

He looks at me like he can barely remember who I am let alone what I told him to do. "I don't know," he says clearly puzzled and unaware that we've had a conversation recently.

"Son, I told you to hang up your coat, take out the trash, and make some tea."

His coat fell off the hanger before he closed the closet door but he never noticed it. Then he mixed water and a scoop of lemonade in a coffee cup. He forgot about the trash and went back to the television.

I called him into the kitchen and handed him the bulging trash bag.

"Son, take this to the garage and wake your brother up while you're out there. It's getting dark. He needs to come inside." (I am not a bad mother. That child weighs a ton and he sleeps like a log. He was fine. Besides, I closed the garage door.)

Ivan returned to the house with his brother but he was still carrying the bag of trash. He put it on the floor and went back to the television.

When my husband came off a few minutes later, I spent ten minutes complaining to him about the children. He sipped on the cup of lemonade and ate a sandwich while I was talking. I finally paused and waited for him to respond. Nothing.

"Did you hear me?" I asked.

He looked at me with glassy, bored eyes and said, "Hmm?"

Mighty Moe vs. Mrs. A

Do you ever feel like Jekyll & Hyde?

More than a century ago, Robert Louis Stevenson wrote the classic tale about opposing identities in the same man. In the case of Jekyll & Hyde, there was a good side and an evil side. For most of us (well, some of us) it isn't so much good versus evil as it is perfect versus practical or, OK, good versus naughty but not really illegal.

Take me, for example. There's my ultrafeminist, I'm-everywoman, side. I call her Mighty Moe. Moe thinks that she can do anything, anytime, anywhere, without anyone's help. She believes that if you want something done right, you gotta do it yourself. She is a salesperson's nightmare. She has never bought anything from a stranger on the telephone. She wants statistics and guarantees, not a lovely coffee mug, thank you. Moe likes a challenge.

Then there's my softer, gentler side. I call her Mrs. A. She likes the idea of being a full-time homemaker. She hates confrontation and just wants to be loved. Mrs. A likes gardening, and she really wants to do the Christmas shopping in July. She thinks her two sons should have an adorable little sister. We try to keep the lid on Mrs. A. Nevertheless, she insists on offering her advice whenever Mighty Moe wants to do her own thing.

Take, for instance, the other morning when I was a little short on cash and my husband was still fast asleep. His wallet was lying on the dresser with several green bills peeking out of it just begging me to take them out for some adventure. Just as my fingers closed around the brown, leather square, Mrs. A piped in with, "You shouldn't go into his wallet without first asking for permission. You know how you are about your purse."

"But he's asleep," replied Mighty Moe. "Why wake him up just to ask for a measly five bucks? He'll just tell her to go ahead and take it like he always does."

Mrs. A is such a pain. She had to go hop up onto her moral soapbox and start preaching. "Remember, do unto others..."

So I took $10 and left him a note.

Mighty Moe could pass by all the solicitors in front of the grocery store without a second glance. Mrs. A is a sucker for any rumpled kid with a carton of melted, stale chocolate bars. She would order cookies from every Girl Scout in the city if she could.

Yesterday, I said to my husband, "Honey, can I use the truck today? I've got to pick up a bunch of office supplies."

As I backed out of the driveway, Mrs. A just had to give me grief.

"You should tell him that your car is on empty."

"He'll figure it out. Besides there's only a fourth of a tank in here," Moe said in my defense.

"Do you really need a truck to carry staples and a bottle of Wite Out or is it just that you're too lazy to stop at a gas station?"

Moe and me were getting fed up with Mrs. A.

"Look, it has nothing to do with laziness. It's a hundred degrees out here. That pump handle is hot and the fumes give me a headache. So just shut up already will ya?

That evening, my husband asked me if I had known that I was out of gas.

"Really!" I said as if I was surprised by this revelation. "I filled up a few days ago."

That was true.

Mrs. A cooked him a big dinner and served it on real dishes instead of paper plates. All was forgiven.

It's a tough task trying to reconcile these two very different personalities and not talk to myself out loud. It's a problem for men and women. For guys, it's often the difficult choice between the hunter-protector and the nurturing-sensitive guy. A constant tug of war. So what do we do when our emotional crossroads start looking like the freeway Mixmaster?

Mrs. A. says, "Always take the high ground and do your very best."

Moe says, "Forget it. Let's just call in sick today."

Mom, Are You Busy?

Not very long ago, I had a problem. This one, particular guy idolized me so much that he constantly followed me around everywhere I went.

Day and night, there he was like a bad haircut. This fellow was relentless! He peered through windows. He spied on me through keyholes. He listened in on my phone conversations. Once, I even caught him rifling through my purse.

I tried talking to him and reasoning with him but to no avail. We couldn't call the police because–well, it would have been embarrassing. The last straw fell when I woke up one morning to find him standing next to my bed, staring at me through the darkness, and breathing hard.

"Take your thumb out of your mouth and go back to bed," I mumbled from beneath the covers to my 4-year old devoted fan. "Didn't Mommy tell you to knock before you come in here?   What time is it anyway?"

"The big hand is on the 12 and the little hand is on the 6," he offered hopefully. "Is it time to go to the zoo?"

Learning how to tell time is pointless until children understand that certain hours and days are for sleeping. Saturday at 6 AM. is one of those days.

"Sweetie, the animals are still sleeping. They don't like to get up early on the weekend. We can't go to the zoo until "The Muppet Babies" come on TV, OK? Now why don't you go and watch cartoons? Let Mommy know when it's time to go."

"I'm hungry."

"I put the Cocoa Puffs on the table last night. Just for this special day, you can sit on the sofa and eat them right out of the box. Don't worry about crumbs or anything. Just go in the den and have a ball. I'll cook you some pancakes when the little hand reaches the 8."

I closed my eyes and hoped to recapture my dream. I was waiting to here the carpet crunch beneath his little feet as he left the room. He didn't budge. I could feel him hovering there, just waiting for any signs of life from me.

"Sweetie, run along now," I said, suppressing a twinge of guilt. "Close the door behind you."

Nothing. He wouldn't go away. He never did, but that didn't stop me from trying. After a few suspenseful moments, he used one little, wet finger to pry open my right eye.

"Mommy, I want you to watch TV with me."

My tired eye tried to focus but it couldn't. I could smell fresh Oreos on his breath. Great, he's already had breakfast. I won't have to cook.

I don't like cartoons. I didn't like cartoons when I was a kid. It didn't matter. I picked him up and plopped him down in the middle of the bed next to his father. Dad hadn't moved the entire time. I know he was faking because he's a light sleeper. I don't blame him. Once you talk to these kids, you have to feed them.

For the rest of the morning, we watched cartoons. My son snuggled up against me, and his warm body shook as he laughed and giggled. I tried not to doze off, but a couple of times, my eyes insisted on closing for a moment. My son would catch me napping and say, "Look Mommy. You're not looking."

That was a few years ago, back when thunder and lightning meant a sleepover in my room. That was before he could cook his own breakfast or ride a bike with no hands. Now, I'm just an accessory to his busy life: the cheerleader, the taxi driver, the doctor, the bank...

Still, every now and then, there's a soft knock on my bedroom door followed by: "Mom, are you busy?"

Now, I'm never too busy for these special moments when he sits on the edge of the bed and shares his thoughts with me and sometimes, as he starts to leave, I'll ask him, "Do you want to watch TV with me?"

"Nah, Mom, maybe another time. I've got some other things I need to do right now," he says.

Then he leaves and he closes the door behind him.

Museum House

They have lovely works of art at the Kimbell Museum in Fort Worth. There are beautiful paintings, specimens, and unusual objects on display throughout the building. Many people travel great distances to view their latest exhibit. It's well worth the trip.

As a child, one of my favorite pastimes was visiting museums like the Amon Carter Museum and the Fort Worth Museum of Science and History. Yes, I was a strange kid.

I carried my love for museums from my parents' home right into my own home.

I don't know exactly how it happened. It all started normally enough with comfortable furnishings purchased more for their practicality and durability than their esthetic value. A couple of episodes of Martha Stewart and a few articles in some decorating magazines changed all of that.

Before you knew it, I started buying frames that cost more than the picture inside them. We had white chairs in the dining room. The rug was a work of art. The magazines - the socially conscious and incredibly boring magazines - were arranged symmetrically on the fingerprint-free table. I was warning my children not to use the "good" soap or the "good" towels in the "good" bathroom.

Eventually, I had to take my shoes off to walk into my own house. I don't even have to remove my shoes at the Kimbell and they've got Cezanne and Matisse in there. We had a dining room that we hardly ever dined in because we might stain the white chairs. And we had a living room that no one lived in.

Like a museum, our house was on display.

People behave a certain way in museums. What's appropriate for a museum is not appropriate for a home. Homes are for living, lounging, loving and laughing.

If the pictures, chairs, towels, and pretty dishes aren't for your family, then who are they for? And why? That's what I asked myself one day when I found myself becoming angry because there was dirt on one of the "good" towels.

I didn't like the answer that I gave myself.

So now, we burn the candles and we use the soap. We drink tap water out of the long-stemmed glasses. Life is too short. The only thing irreplaceable in my home is my family.

You know, I still love to visit museums. I just don't want to live in one.

Parties Are For Guests

Why can't they just understand, comprehend, or simply get it? Why, why, why must I endure this torment from my family every six to eight months? Where is the love? Where is the understanding? Where is the furniture polish?

Yes, I'm having a party, a bridal shower to be exact. In just a few hours, 30 to 40 of my dearest, closest, almost-perfect friends are going to descend upon my residence to help me celebrate the pending nuptials of my one and only little sister.

I am a nervous wreck.

There is so much to do! It's not just getting the invitations out and preparing hors durves or whatever. I hate that word. I always misspell it and I don't have time to look it up. I'm too busy planning this party. I'm talking about preparing snacks, OK! Anyway, it's not the standard ice bucket and centerpieces stuff that makes entertaining an ordeal. Rather, it's the behind the scenes stuff. You know, the toilet cleaning, furniture polishing, and strategic camouflage.

I have stuffed papers, bills and all the other junk that's usually lying around on the counters into every drawer and cabinet that I thought no one could possibly have a reason to open during the shower. I've cleaned the baseboards and dusted the blinds. I've washed the walls and Windexed the windows. I even sat in every chair so that I could see my guests' view and make sure that no spider web or stray crumb was in sight.

And in truth, my husband has been quite helpful. The yard is beautiful, every weed uprooted and the hedges are symmetrical. He's moved the furniture around half a dozen times and right now he's looking for that extra piece that makes the table wider.

But goodness, these children of mine are doing their best to prevent me from entering hostess heaven. I heard them grumbling about me earlier to day.

"Mom sounds like an owl doesn't she? Every few minutes she says, Who? Who? Who?"

Well, what am I supposed to say when they eat the beautiful fruit that I bought specifically for the guests' viewing pleasure?

"Who ate one of the green apples? Didn't I tell you guys that this fruit is for display?"

And when I went into the bathroom by the den, someone had actually used the soap and splashed water on the mirror!

"Who used this bathroom?" I yelled to no one in particular. "Didn't you see the Porta Potty that I rented? It's right there by the driveway."

"But Mom, we thought that was for your friends to use."

"Goodness no! I wouldn't let my friends go in there. That's for you. There's even a comic book in there and a can of Lysol. Now don't go in the good bathroom again until the party is over."

"But Mom," they protest, "you said that our house is not a museum and you want it to be a place where we can enjoy ourselves. What happened to that?"

"That was before this party came up. For the next two days, our house is the Smithsonian, OK? Don't touch a thing and do not enter the roped off areas. Now go next door. The neighbors should be eating dinner about now. Look hungry when they come to the door. Hang around a while after you eat and remember to leave your shoes in the garage when you come back."

I know. This is way off the deep end and totally unnecessary but I don't care. People are coming to my home and by golly, that garage is going to be dust free before they get here. That's just the way it is.

Later, I'll get therapy. Right now, I've got things to do.

Farewell My Jeans

This is the end of an era. This is my swan song to youth. This is the day that I've dreaded since my high school principal handed me my diploma and said, "Welcome to the real world."

The real world stinks.

How much more can I bear? I've given up so much already in my efforts to be a good wife, a good mother, and a productive citizen. I've already given up short shorts and mini skirts. I've stopped going to happy hour after work. I drive the posted speed limit (most of the time) wear my seat belt (all of the time.) Sometimes, I eat vegetables that I don't even like.   And really, with all the advances in genetic engineering, can't they make lettuce have some sort of flavor? Forget the speckled roses; give us Brussels Sprouts that taste like chocolate or strawberry.

Anyway, the point is that I've made a lot of sacrifices in my efforts to transform my baser pediatric nature into grown-up material. But now a demand is being made of me that I simply cannot accept. Not this. Not now.

It all started with my annual clearing out of the closets. Following the tradition of my mother, I scour the clothes vaults in our home diligently seeking out torn, faded, outdated clothing which I then pass on to my youngest child. No, not really. Well, not the badly torn stuff. The kid's gotta have some play clothes though.

Of course, it's pretty easy to figure out which items the children need to part with and as long as I do it while they're away ~ no problem. The problem comes with my husband and me. He wants to keep that Super Fly collar, psychedelic shirt until it comes back into style and I want to keep my button fly blue jeans until they fit again.

"That's not going to happen," he says skeptically as I remove my jeans from the pile designated for Goodwill.

"It's going to happen sooner than that shirt sees the light of day," I retort.

"Why can't you just accept that you're not a size 5 anymore and throw those jeans away?"

"This is baby fat. I just had a child recently and soon I'm going to lose this extra weight and my feet are going to return to their original size."

"Your baby is 9 years old and we're not even going to discuss your feet."

He just doesn't understand.

Those jeans are my last link to the carefree, washboard stomach days of my youth. If I give up the jeans, I'm admitting that I'll never again eat pancakes at three in the morning and not get indigestion. Worse than that even, I'll be resigning myself to shopping only in the women's department where they don't play videos and all the mannequins look like they just had a plate of dry lettuce for dinner.

"No," I say, "I can't do it. I won't give up the jeans. I'm not saying that they won't get dusty again before I can wear them but I promise you, I'll wear these jeans before you wear that shirt."

My husband disappears into the other room and comes back a moment later carrying a fashion magazine. Inside is a young, male model dancing under a marquee that says "The Color of Success" and wearing a shirt that looks remarkably like my spouse's.

I smile in defeat and then I put my jeans back into the closet. I don't care. I'm not giving up on those jeans - not yet anyway.

Big Mama

The hysterical screams of the chickens woke us up around midnight. The darkness was so thick that you could slice it with a butcher's knife. My small body trembled and rolled toward my grandmother's side of the bed as she abruptly sat up and moved to the edge of the mattress.

In the air, the odious growl of a hungry wolf echoed strangely off-key in the squawking chorus. I held my breath and followed the sound of my grandmother's footsteps as she walked to the corner by the fireplace and picked up her .22-caliber rifle.

"Stay here, Monica!" she commanded in her heavy alto as she headed towards the porch at the back of the house. Naturally, I jumped out of the bed and followed on her heels as closely as I dared. I feared the dark more than I feared her reproach. She didn't turn on any lights as she made her way through the house. I couldn't reach the strings hanging from the naked bulbs high above me.

We emerged from the dark house into the black night like a female version of The Lone Ranger and Tonto, but this Tonto was terrified. My Grandmother never paused for breath. She raised the rifle barrel up to her shoulder and pumped off three rounds before I could plug my ears. Her face glowed like a strange earth angel each time the long barrel belched out fire and smoke. She was aiming so high that I didn't think she'd hit the barn, let alone some crazy wolf. Later I realized that she wasn't actually trying to hit anything. She just wanted to frighten the wolf away. The chickens were so scared that they didn't lay any eggs for a few days.

My Uncle Raymond, one of her 15 children, killed a cow one time when he was deer hunting. He can't see very well. Of course, it was broad daylight then, but the point is that you have to be careful around the livestock.

The next morning I awakened to the oh-so-wonderful smell of homemade biscuits, fresh sausage, and scrambled eggs. My Grandmother never even mentioned the previous night. If it weren't for the bloody fur on the barbed wire near the hen house, I would have thought it was all a dream. She was some kind of woman, my grandma.

She passed away a year ago today. It's funny how the memories seem more vivid than ever even after all this time. She was so strong and wise and patient. She survived so much tragedy, poverty and racism. After the slaves were emancipated, my ancestors walked from Arkansas to East Texas and built the homestead outside Jefferson, where my Grandmother lived until she passed away. Everything she could see from her back porch belonged to her.

Always the optimist, she never complained, and she never looked back with regret. She walked again after the first stroke and left the doctors shaking their heads in wonder.

Then the last years brought the heart attack, cancer, another stroke and so many brown bottles of medicine from so many doctors. By the time she went away, it was a merciful alternative to the life of total dependency that she'd never had and never wanted.

I knew it was coming, but you just can't prepare for that sort of pain. I cried a lot at first. Time is a good pain reliever but it tends to wear off abruptly, just like aspirin.

It wore off today. I woke up this morning, and the sadness washed over me like a steamy shower of tears. I thought I was beyond this harshest form of grief. I thought I could live the rest of my life content with all my happy memories of our time together. And I can. Except ~ every now and then, when some unexpected event ~ a sight, the sound of someone's voice, or the smell of hot biscuits ~ opens a floodgate of blue emotions that no amount of reason can control.

She's not suffering anymore. She had a long, productive life. She wouldn't have been happy confined to a bed. I know, yes, I know. Those are logical, reasonable answers but hearts won't listen to logic. Not mine anyway. Hearts just love... Right now, I really miss my Grandma.

Invisible Fred

"F-R-D."

That's exactly what he wrote in his large, childish scrawl. The "E" was missing and the other big, red letters were a slanted downhill. His "R" looked more like a "P" but overall, for a 3-year-old, it was pretty good penmanship. If I hadn't been so furious with my little Frederick, I would have been proud of his academic achievement.

"Frederick Cecil Martin Anderson!" I yelled at the top of my lungs. "You get in here right now, young man!"

He sheepishly peeped around the corner from the den where he was watching a Barney video.

"Yes, my pretty Mommy?" he asked innocently.

"Fred, did you write your name on the dining room wall with this red crayon?"

I showed him the broken pieces of Crayola that I'd found laying on the carpet nearby.

He looked at the wall and he looked at the crayon as if he'd never seen them before in his life. His eyes widened and he put his pudgy little hands on his pudgy little cheeks.

"No pretty Mommy. Not me. I didn't do it."

Determined not to laugh or succumb to his toddler charms, I continued my interrogation. "Well son, I sure didn't do it. Who do you suppose did this?"

"Daddy?" he offered hopefully. Even at that tender age he could naively insult my intelligence.

"Daddy is out of town son, and Daddy's name is not Fred."

"Maybe the bad man did it. He took my color and wrote on Mommy's nice wall. You should give the bad man time out, Mommy."

"Fred, why on earth would someone break into our house and write your name on this egg-shell white wall?"

"I dunno," he said sadly and shook his little head. He seemed genuinely at a loss for a reasonable explanation of the graffiti burglar's neurotic behavior.

When and where do these children learn to fib? From the time my sons began to seek and destroy, they have been trying to stay out of trouble by deceiving me. We had an "invisible dog" that kept leaving the refrigerator door open. The "cookie fairy" loved to raid our cookie jar and sprinkle crumbs all over the countertop. And dear old "Idunno" breaks something that I love dearly at least once a month.

When "Idunno" doesn't work, they blame each other.

No one ever wants to take responsibility for their actions. I've told them that honesty is the best policy. I've tried to get them to understand that the consequences of truth are not as severe as the consequences of their falsehoods.

I thought I was making headway until something really strange happened last weekend.

I had a rare, glorious weekend alone. The boys were at sleepovers and my husband was away on business. I spent Friday evening in bed reading a love story and eating an entire bowl of popcorn by myself. I went to sleep at 9 o' clock and I didn't stir again until 9 AM the next day. Oh joy, joy.

That morning, I sat up in bed and stretched, then I blinked several times and rubbed my eyes. I couldn't believe what I saw before me! Someone had taken my favorite red lipstick and written a message on the mirror over the dresser.

It said, "Have a nice day, love Frd."

My Sister's Parents

You should meet my sister's parents. They are so great.

They're open-minded, flexible and patient as the day is long.
They are just incredible. I only have one sibling, my younger sister.
More than a decade lies between us. I don't know what happened
during that long childbearing break, but she is so lucky to have
those cool folks.

In fact, she's getting married soon and she's asked me to be the
matron of honor. I hate that word "matron." It sounds so– so–old.
I asked her if I could be the "head bridesmaid" or "leader of the
pack," but she said no. My dictionary tells me that a matron is a
mature, dignified married woman. Under the circumstances, I've
gotta wear those dyed-to-match shoes, even if they don't fit well.

Anyway, I had good parents, too. They were there for me when
I needed them. They provided shelter, clothing and helped me with
my homework. They even played Monopoly with me until I had a
hotel on every property and they couldn't get past "Go." But they
were just a little uptight at times as they tried to figure out the best
way to raise their first child. We broke a lot of new ground together.

In fact, my parents are a lot like my sister's parents. They look
just like them, so much so that it's uncanny at times. They sound
like them, and they even live in the same house with the same
phone number. If I were not so perceptive, I would be misled into
thinking that they were the same people. But I know that some
alien life forms have taken my parents away and left these kinder,
gentler people in their stead.

It's the little things that give them away. For example, my sister
sleeps until 10 on some Saturday mornings. When I call for her,
her mother says, "Oh, she's tired, so I'm letting her sleep in."

What? She's tired! When did that become an issue? I had to
get up with the roosters every Saturday and start housecleaning. No
one cared if I was tired after Friday night football and burgers. I

did more by 10 AM than she does all day. Am I jealous? You bet your feather duster I am.

Another time, we were planning a big family vacation, and my mother made a suggestion about the destination. My sister vehemently disagreed, and do you know what happened?

Mom said, "OK, Jaye, tell us your ideas. Let's try to work out a compromise that's a win-win situation for all of us."

I do not know this person.

Before it was always, no money ~ no vote. This new democracy is unfamiliar to me. I'm not saying that I don't like it, I'm just having trouble becoming accustomed to it.

The good thing about this situation is that my sister's parents are also my children's grandparents. My boys think the sun rises and sets on those two.

They let them eat whatever they want within reason. They actually watch cartoons with the boys. And since Grandpa retired, he has a lot more time for after school activities and he's always available in the event of an emergency.

Yessir, my sister's folks are definitely keepers. I wouldn't change a thing about them.

And the best part is - they let me call them "Mom" and "Dad" too.

Parent-Teacher Conference

"Mom, my teacher wants to talk to you."

"No! No! A thousand times No!" scream the legion of voices in my head.

But instead of dissolving into a puddle of anxiety before my impressionable baby child, I smile at him and calmly say, "Really? Why does your teacher want to talk to me."

He shrugs. "I dunno. Maybe it's about me being so smart that they want me to skip a grade."

Reflecting on his last report card, I have serious doubts that his genius IQ will be the topic of conversation. You know there's a problem when the teacher wants a conference. No one is going to ask you to take time off work and come to the school just so they can tell you that you have a great kid.

Besides, I already knew what they were going to tell me. It's the same thing they tell me every year. Usually, I'm summoned before the first six weeks are up. This time we made it halfway through the year. I guess that's progress. Basically, my son talks too much, and he likes to clown around. He's the same way at home. We've tried everything to make him focus and be more serious but to no avail. So here we go again.

On the designated day, I found myself seated in a kid-size chair with my thighs peering over the side looking for gum beneath the seat.

The first teacher said, "I want you to know how much I enjoy having your son in my class. He's a great kid."

I thanked her and braced myself for the 'however' part.

"He's very popular with the other children. He has great social skills," she continued.

That's nice teacher lingo for "He talks too much."

The second teacher spoke up. "We're just concerned that he's not applying himself. He gets his work done but he doesn't always give it his complete focus. We think he could do better."

That means, "He doesn't have an attention deficit disorder, he just talks too much."

The meeting went on a while but ultimately, it boiled down to, "He talks too much." I pledged to work together with the teachers to improve my son's performance in the classroom. We discussed various techniques, from points to prizes to reward positive behavior. When the meeting was done, I stood, brushed the carpet lint off my hips and thanked the teachers for their time and dedication toward educating the youth of our country.

Later that evening, my husband and I, talked with my son about the meeting. My son crossed his heart and pledged to turn over a new leaf.

After he left the room, my husband asked, "Do you think he'll make it until summer?"

"I don't know. I averaged two conferences a year until high school."

"You're kidding! Ms. Law & Order got into trouble?"

"Well, I–"

"Don't tell me," he said. "You talked too much right?"

Spastic Colon

My family went to Houston for a New Year's Eve party. As we were driving back, I was conked out in the back seat with my youngest son. My husband was driving, and my oldest child was beside him, reading a book with some mutant, green-faced child on the cover.

My deep slumber ended abruptly when I felt the first of many pains to come rip through my stomach like a sickle. Prepare yourselves for this. I have a spastic colon. I don't know if it's proper etiquette to say this out loud, but that's what it's called. Anyway, I prefer that name to "irritable bowel syndrome." Who wants a colon with a funky attitude?

When my intestines get testy, they spasm until I'm doubled over in agony. Childbearing women can relate this feeling to labor pains. The rest of you should just imagine being repeatedly kicked in the stomach with a combat boot.

I hadn't had an attack in almost a year, so I wasn't prepared for this one. After I had moaned and groaned for five minutes, my husband finally said: "What's the matter with you? Is your stomach thing bothering you again?"

"I don't have my pills," I hissed through clenched teeth. I doubled over and rolled on the floor of the car.

Everyone was oddly silent for a few miles. My baby boy stared out of the window apparently counting cows. It was as if they could not even hear my sounds of distress. I know that they are not deaf. They always hear me when I say, "Dinner is ready!"

My big boy finally spoke. "Mom, will you please stop bumping into my seat? I can't read."

Thanks, son.

My husband finally asked if I wanted to go to the hospital. I told him no. Eventually the pain goes away. Eventually was just taking a long time this time. Besides, I didn't want to go through the HMO nightmare of making an emergency visit to a nonparticipating hospital. Then I felt the car make a U-turn, and I screamed at my husband: "Where are you going? Just take me home! I want to go home!"

He ignored my theatrics, as usual. "I'm taking you to the hospital," he said, continuing to drive 55 mph.

Tears coursed down my face. My little boy glanced at me, horrified, and grabbed his action figure off the seat next to me. He carefully wiped my tears from the doll's plastic purple cape. I think that was his way of offering me sympathy.

My husband frowned into the rearview mirror. "Look," he said, "we can't ride another three hours with you carrying on like that." I'm sure that was his way of saying: "Honey, I'm worried about you. You're in a lot of pain, and it hurts me to see you suffer."

He even sped up a bit. I think at one point the speedometer made it all the way to 60.

We were 10 miles from the hospital when the pain disappeared as suddenly as it had come. I sat up, dried my face and put my seat belt back on.

"Take me home," was all I said.

My husband turned the car around and headed for Arlington.

My baby and his one-armed action figure smiled at me. Junior finally turned the page in that engrossing book of his.

My husband relaxed his death grip on the steering wheel and stopped grinding his teeth. We all breathed again.

These macho men don't fool me. They love me - in their own special way.

And in mine, I love them, too.

Pumpkin Head

I probably should keep it to myself, but really, it's nothing to be ashamed of: I have a large head.

It's not monstrous to the point that people on the street stop and stare, but it's large enough to prevent me from buying hats at the department store. I made this important discovery in the fourth grade, the year that Joshua O'Leary started his annual Fat Head contest.

He confiscated a tape measure from his mother's sewing kit and brought it to school in his lunch box. During lunch, he proposed, "Let's measure everybody and see who has the biggest head."

Apparently, math class had inspired him. Anyway, we were all sure that Big Mack would win. Mack liked the fourth grade so much that he was repeating it for the second time.

He was very popular because he told us what would be on the test, and he was real good at baseball. Sure enough, Big Mack was winning by a country mile until they came to the last contestant, a small girl at the end of the table.

That would be me.

Imagine my surprise when I beat Mack by a good two inches! No one ever beat Mack at anything. That was an honor I could have done without.

I smiled weakly as Joshua placed a cereal bowl on my head and said, "I now crown you the Fourth Grade Fat Head," and everyone cheered like crazy until the cafeteria monitor yelled at us and threatened to take our green Jell-O.

My best friend spent the rest of the day defending me from all the teasing.

"She doesn't have a fat head! She has a huge brain, and it needs a lot of room," she said.

I arrived home in tears and ran to my mother's side. "Mama, do I have a big head? Everybody says I have a big head."

She looked genuinely surprised to hear this news. She examined my head and concluded, "No precious, your head is just perfect.

It's not too big or too small. Whoever said that didn't know what they were talking about."

Then she kissed the top of my big head and gave me ice cream.

She had to do that every year until junior high school when big Afros became vogue and Joshua moved to Wisconsin to help his grandpa make cheese.

I suppose mama knew I had a big head since she often called me pumpkin, but then again, love is blind.

I know my kids have a few blemishes but I have to focus real hard to see them. I'd hate to have a parent who didn't think I was the greatest thing ever.

I heard a woman call her kid a stupid idiot in the mall the other day. He didn't even flinch. I guess she says that a lot. If children don't leave home with a lot of self-confidence and self-esteem, they will never acquire any in a world full of Joshua O'Learys.

There are so many people outside of our families anxious to ridicule us and point out our imperfections for the world to see. I figure misery loves company and do my best to leave them lonely.

When my own little pumpkin has a bad day, we talk about what he needs to do to make improvements and then I reassure him with a big hug. I say, "Sweetie, you're the greatest. Don't give out and don't give up. I love you just the way you are."

Then I kiss him on his head that's shaped exactly like mine– and we have ice cream.

Road Rage

My cousin LouBerta is sweet as can be, but frankly, she's two cans short of a six-pack, if you know what I mean.

Her real name is Flossie Mae. She says that name sounds too uppity so we just call her LouBerta. We're allowed to do that kind of thing in the South. LouBerta insists on living alone. Her doctor says that she's stable, but sometimes I wonder.

It never fails that LouBerta reads a headline in the paper and flies off the handle without reading the whole story. For example, when she heard about this "Road Rage" phenomenon happening all over the country, she hopped into her canary yellow Ford F-150 pickup and headed over to Home Depot where she purchased a bunch of lumber and some long nails.

She knew that she couldn't stop something like this road rage with a weapon or simple reasoning. Nope, she decided to just board up all her doors and windows instead.

When we arrived at her home for our monthly visit, she asked my husband to help her unload the plywood sheets from her truck.

"What is all this wood for, LouBerta?" he asked as he placed the wood where she directed.

"I'm fixin' to board up the house like they did in that movie, 'The Birds'," she replied.

He was quiet for a few minutes. Aunt LouBerta gets mad kind of easily so he spoke each word carefully and slowly when he asked, "Why are you boarding up the house?"

"Pass me the hammer, please," she responded as she climbed a ladder and tried to explain with nails between her teeth. "Don't y'all read the paper? The roads and highways are in a rage! They're killing folks all over the country! I'm trying to protect myself and you should do the same."

No one but Stephen King and Cousin LouBerta would have ever dreamed of the day when the very streets we drive on, mercilessly day and night, would rise and take their revenge; those long, menacing, strips of tar miraculously sprouting arms, legs, and fangs and breaking into her home to terrorize her throughout the night.

No one laughed. Goodness knows we wanted to, but that's very impolite.

"Cousin LouBerta," I explained, "the roads are not angry. Road rage is about aggressive drivers. You know, those rude people who cut you off on the freeway, tailgate and run red lights. That kind of stuff. Road rage is just a catchy new name for reckless driving. The police are trying to stop it so they can reduce the number of traffic accidents. It's nothing to be afraid of."

"Oh," she said kind of quiet like. "You mean there aren't any psycho roads throwing drivers off bridges and smashing their cars with telephone poles?"

"I'm afraid not."

She climbed down from the ladder and walked over to the pile of wood.

"I believe I'll build me a gazebo," she said. "Y'all want some of my ginger tea and sweet potato pie?"

"Yes ma'am, that sounds mighty good."

We didn't visit Cousin LouBerta as long as we usually do. I insisted on leaving before dark. Not that I believed her wild tale about the roads and all. But you never know.

Sexual Thoughts

According to S. Freud, men, both married and single, think about sex a dozen or more times a day. Women, especially married women with children like me, are far less likely to think about sex. Freud says that we average one fleeting thought a day unless we're on vacation in which case we equal the men.

That's Sherman Freud, by the way. He's the guy that delivers the bottled water to my office. He was right about the Cowboys and the Vikings last week so I'll at least entertain the thought.

After pondering this baffling statistic for a while, I decided to closely monitor my thoughts for an entire day just to see if Freud was right. I chose a Monday because I'm still fresh then and, therefore, most likely to have fresh thoughts.

6 AM: Rise and shine. OK-just rise. Put on robe and make coffee. Wake children. Husband is gone; can't remember where he went. Oh, well. Drink coffee. Go to work.

8 AM: Start work. Act friendly, help people. Wonder what to eat for lunch. Admire assistant's new hairstyle. Room is hot. Adjust thermometer. Count days until next vacation.

Noon: Go to Mexican restaurant. Order Greek salad with French dressing. Waiter is attractive, nice cologne, tight jeans. Almost think of sex then remember that youngest son needs new jeans. Grow like weeds. Eat salad and make grocery list.

2 PM: Call spouse at work. He says, "Hey baby, what's up?" Flashback to college days when he always called me "baby." Feel warm and fuzzy momentarily, then I remember labor pains. Ask husband to bring home bread and chips. Hang up.

5 PM: Drive home and change into something comfortable. Help with homework while cooking dinner. Open mail, return calls, read newspaper. Read about sex but have no independent thoughts about the subject.

10 PM: Prepare for bed. Think about sex while brushing teeth. Husband is watching Monday night football and yelling at the television. Not romantic. Crush thought and go to bed.

12 AM-Midnight: Did not hear spouse enter room or come to bed. Hear son scratch his ear and shiver in his bedroom. Get up, wash son's ear, apply cortisone, and put extra blanket on him. Climb over husband, fluff pillow, go back to sleep.

6 AM: Rise.

Gosh, I guess ole Sherman's on to something. Just to make sure that I wasn't weird, I called several friends of various ages, races, and professions. Friends assured me that I'm normal and possibly above average. No one had an explanation for the thought drought.

Everyone updated me on their children's latest accomplishments and their horrendous workload. We concluded that thinking about romance is just another responsibility like paying bills or balancing the checkbook. It should be assigned to one spouse so that there is no confusion and things don't get out of hand.

Wait, I think I'm about to have one of those thoughts. Nah, it was just gas. Gotta get a Tums.

Snake In the Garage

They say truth is stranger than fiction and I don't doubt it for a minute. If you ever run out of excuses to explain why you were late for work, I've got a brand new one for you. Tell them, "There was a snake in the garage, and I couldn't get to my car!" It happened to me and I'm still shaking in my pumps.

One morning, I was getting dressed for work and I told my son to go ahead and put his golf clubs in the trunk because I had to drop him off for his lessons on my way to the office. Two minutes later, he came running into my bedroom shaking and screaming like James Brown: "Snake in the garage! There's a snake in the garage! Mom, there's this huge snake in the garage! I think it's a python! You gotta go look at it," he insisted.

As he is prone to exaggeration, (can't imagine where he got that from) I did not immediately react to his hysterics. I finished applying my lipstick and said, "OK son, I do believe that there's a snake in the garage, but I doubt that it's a python. Pythons don't live in this part of the country and besides, pythons are really huge. It's probably just a garden snake. He's as frightened as you are. He's probably gone by now but if he's still in the garage, we'll just toss him into the grass."

I grabbed a broom before opening the door to the garage and boldly stepped onto the oily concrete prepared to dispense with this nuisance intruder. Out of the corner of my eye, I saw something move by the trashcan. I turned around and saw the longest, fattest, scariest looking snake that I have ever seen outside of a zoo. I screamed, dropped the broom, ran back into the house, and slammed the door.

"Geez! Did you see that thing? I think it's a boa constrictor."

"See, I told you Mom. What are we gonna do? He's right by the car."

"I know. I'm glad I didn't leave the keys in there. He's big enough to drive," I said.

I took a few deep breaths and tried to decide on the best course of action. Having spent much of my youth in the woods of East Texas, I'm no stranger to snakes and such. I pride myself on my courage and resourcefulness. Therefore, I did what any self-respecting new age woman would do in a situation like this.

I called my husband at work and said, "There's a snake in the garage! There's a snake in the garage!"

My knight rushed home to save me from the serpent. Admittedly, he was a little smug when he arrived and first heard our story. He grabbed a garden hoe and started poking around the garage for the "little earthworm". All of a sudden, this huge, hissing head emerged from behind the lawn mower. That sucker was a good 3-feet long. My husband did a triple jump that Carl Lewis would envy.

My son and I chimed, "Told you so."

Thus the battle between man and nature began. Despite my protests, my husband chased the snake all over the garage. I begged him to let the police or someone handle it but he said, "He came into my garage and scared my family. Call whoever you want but he's mine!" I was so afraid that the snake would bite my husband or vice versa that I called 911. When I went back outside, my husband had cornered the snake in the branches of a red tip, and he was trying to spear it with the hoe. My son was a hundred yards away yelling, "Get him Dad!"

Thankfully, the animal control people arrived and snared the snake which they said was some kind of "bull" snake. They promised to take it away to safety and freedom somewhere far, far away.

Of course, no one believed me when I arrived at work an hour late and told them what happened. Meanwhile, I haven't parked in the garage in a week. Did I mention that I was usually inside the house, in the woods of East Texas?

Senior/Rookie Couples

Perchance you were there that day at the restaurant when I dined alone on a spinach salad and water with a stale lemon slice. There was French bread, of course, but that's not the point.

I wonder if you saw them, the two couples, and if you noticed the interesting dynamics that accompanied their meal. I am not an anthropologist so I can only tell you what I saw, but for me it was like viewing a timeline of marriage from it's fresh, raw, anxious origins to the seasoned, well-done, comfortable conclusion.

Couple No. 1, the rookie couple, entered the dining room holding hands, trying to navigate the narrow aisles side by side. They accepted the table by the hot window without question and smiled as they squinted at their menus. The glaring sun beaming through the thick window pane made their faces glow like something ethereal and somewhat repulsive in a Ken and Barbie (Is all that hair real?) way. After a few moments of straining to read the difficult menu selections of a burger, salad or pizza, she told him, "Oh honey, I can't decide. I'm going to the little girls room. Will you order for me?"

A frightened look crossed his face. Was it fear of reading alone or fear that she wouldn't return from the potty? Who knows? But he smiled and said, "OK, be careful." I guess she'd had problems in the bathroom before. When the waiter arrived, the young man ordered two soft drinks and a pizza.

That's when the veteran couple walked in. Single file they came down the aisle. First, the waiter, then the wife with her silver head of perfect hair held straight and high, and finally the husband whose bald head swiveled like a globe as he scanned the restaurant for colleagues and friends.

The waiter led them to a table near the hot window and me.

"My wife can't sit here. It's too warm, and the glare gives her headaches," said the man.

The waiter led them to a table next to me. She put her coat on her chair and said, "Restroom." He nodded without looking at her.

He ordered two cups of hot tea and two Caesar salads without croutons.

When the rookie wife returned, her spouse said, "I ordered you a Coke."

"Diet?"

"Uh, no. Just a regular Coke."

Her face said that she hated regular Coke but her lips said, "Sure, that's fine, Boo. Thank you."

The veterans ate their salads in silence while the rookies shared a pizza and talked about the last episode of Saturday Night Live. Yet, they all looked happy. I wondered if the newlywed intoxication of the one would survive to become the sober contentment of the other.

So many love-struck larvae spin a silk cocoon of homes, children and cars only to emerge years later as two disappointed moths with nothing in common. Then again, a beautiful butterfly with two sets of wings and a common purpose can evolve from those same origins.

"I do," means so much.

As I rose to leave, they all turned to look at me. I smiled. They smiled back. I left. That is all. I can only tell you what I saw.

Sweet Potato Pie

Before television brought us news from around the world, twenty-four hours a day, and the Internet made the oceans seems inconsequential, my perspectives were often as narrow as a plastic straw.

I thought everyone's lifestyle was pretty much the same, give or take a few bedrooms. I thought everyone had the same values as my family. I even thought everyone ate sweet potato pie. Boy, was I ever wrong.

I remember it well. "Yuck! This is the worst sweet potato pie I've ever had!"

That's what I whispered to my husband after I tasted the orange pie our hostess offered us for dessert following a delicious Thanksgiving dinner several years ago.

Then our hostess said, "Would you guys like for me to heat up your pumpkin pie in the microwave?"

"Oh, is that what this is?" I replied. "I thought it was sweet potato pie. I've never had this before."

"Sweet potato pie? That sounds good. You'll have to bake one and let me try it."

I'd be happy to, I thought. You'll kick this stuff to the curb after you try sweet potato pie.

Unfortunately, I had no idea how to make my favorite pie. My grandmother always made them because she made them best. So I called up Grandma and asked for her recipe.

"Well baby," she said. (She started every conversation with that phrase.) "First you get some flour."

"Flour?"

"Yes, for the pie crusts."

"Grandma, I've already bought two-nine inch pie crusts so we can skip that part."

"Well, it won't taste right but that's OK since it's your first time. Alrighty, fix up four medium sweet potatoes."

"Exactly how do I fix 'em up Grandma?"

"Boil 'em child. Ain't you got no sense at all?

"Yes ma'am. Boil the potatoes. OK, then what?"

"Then you blend the potatoes with four eggs, a stick of butter, a small can of evaporated milk, and let me think, oh yeah, a little vanilla."

"How much is 'a little' Grandma?"

"Girl, are you trying to cook this by yourself? I don't believe you're ready for solo cooking. Do you know how to work the oven?"

"I'm married with children, Grandma. I can do it. How much vanilla do I need precisely?"

"A couple of teaspoons, I reckon. And then you put a dash of cinnamon and a smidgen of cloves."

I didn't even ask.

She continued, "Blend it all up until it's smooth and bake it around 375 degrees for 45-50 minutes. Stick a toothpick in the center to see if it's done."

"What will the toothpick do, turn orange or something?"

"Baby, let Grandma just mail you a pie."

Half an hour later, I had peeled, cubed, boiled, and blended but something just didn't seem right. The pie mix wasn't sweet enough. Grandma didn't mention sugar so I didn't add any. I thought the heat must bring out the natural sweetness in the potatoes or something like that. Wrong.

I called Grandma and said, "Grandma, was I supposed to put sugar in this pie? It's not very sweet."

She laughed and said, "Baby, you know Grandma is forgetful sometimes. That's why the Lord gave you common sense."

"OK Grandma. I love you."

"I love you, too, baby and don't you throw that pie away. Wasting good food is a sin. Just put some whip cream on it and tell 'em it's pumpkin pie."

Tanning Salon

Boy, oh boy, I tell you it was simply terrifying. Nothing I've ever done, not even skydiving, was as frightening as what happened that evening.

There I was crouched down in a corner in my sweaty birthday suit trembling like a leaf with this blinding light surrounding me. I couldn't see or hear anything, and all I could feel was unbridled fear and the broken glass beneath my feet. Too embarrassed to call out for help. I just sat there helplessly and waited for the world to end. Fortunately, it didn't, but that is definitely the last time I go to a tanning salon.

No, it wasn't my idea. I know nothing about intentionally tanning. When we go to the beach, my husband and I are under an umbrella or a shady tree. Not that I don't enjoy the sun, but I have a nice tan already. My dermatologist suggested it to help with a skin condition.

The staff at the place was very nice and they didn't even act surprised to see me. I was given a tour of the facilities. I looked for peepholes and made sure the doors locked while they demonstrated their disinfection techniques.

They gave me two warnings: One, don't tan for more than twenty minutes. Two, don't look at the lights in the tanning bed because it will damage your eyes. They even gave me some weird goggles to wear in case I was tempted to take a peek.

After locking the door and putting a chair under the knob, I prepared for this groundbreaking experience. I thought I'd start with just ten minutes since it was my first time. After programming the machine, I climbed into the tanning bed, donned my goggles, and turned it on.

Immediately the questions started jostling in my head. What if the timer isn't working properly? Can I get skin cancer from doing this? Is anyone watching me? How do I turn this thing off if I want to get out? Paranoia oozed through my body and shoved anxiety through my pores as I lay there afraid to move.

It seemed like I'd been lying there forever when I heard the first beep. I remembered the staff person telling me, "The machine will beep when your time is halfway through and then again at the end." Good the machine must be working properly, I thought. Although, it seemed like I'd been lying there at least a half-hour already.

The heat started to get to me. My mild claustrophobia kicked in. I heard a beep and my eyes flew open. The lights were still on! I panicked and pushed the top of the tomblike bed open. The goggles fell off and with my eyes clamped shut, I fumbled around with the machine trying to turn it off but I couldn't. I stumbled around blindly groping for my clothes and that's when I stepped on my eyeglasses. I found a sweatshirt and wrapped it around my head. I made it to the corner by the door and squatted down with my back to the machine.

That's when it hit me. It was Wednesday, April 1 and that Taiwanese guy in Garland said that God was coming back today! Please don't let this be it. I know it doesn't matter but I was kind of hoping to be dressed when that happens.

Just when I'd given up hope and was about to yell out for help, the machine turned off. I looked around the room sheepishly, hoping I hadn't missed a peephole.

That's when I saw the fly on the wall. He was laughing so hard that he fell off and started rolling around, kicking his stupid little feet in the air. He was still laughing when I left.

The Buttocks Booster

Reunions. Now I know why some people don't attend. The five-year "I Can't Afford These Clothes But I Wanted To Impress You" reunion wasn't so bad. We still wore the same size shoes, and we were optimistic about the future. But 10 years, now that's a different story altogether.

We have 10 years worth of bills, babies, and bulges smothering our youthful optimism. Our feet are a half size larger and our mortgages have tripled. We realize that even if we do pay off that student loan someday, we will never be debt-free. Yeah, 10 years is when reality hits you with a two-by-four and it doesn't even hurt because you've been hit so many times before.

So am I going to my 10-year class reunion? Heck yeah! I wouldn't miss it for the world. See I've come up with an invention that is going to change everyone's attitudes about reunions and other public gatherings. This invention is going to be so hot that it will make the lava lamp pale in comparison.

Unfortunately, too much of our self-esteem is centered on our appearance. We inflict even more vicious scrutiny upon ourselves whenever we are going to be reunited with people from our distant past. Well we can't reverse the effects of time, but we can reverse the effects of gravity.

"How?" you ask. It's simple, really.

I've come up with a little device that will give you back your youthful figure or at least some of it anyway. It's called the "Buttocks Booster." Yes, a brassiere for your behind.

Don't laugh. I'm serious.

I've put a lot of thought into this. They've got things for women that push-up, lift and separate. We even have straps attached so we can heave-ho all we want until we're as perky as a maid. Why should this technology be limited to women?

Voila! I give you underpants with two adjustable straps that extend from your waist, up and over each shoulder. For tight blue jeans, you simply apply a lot of tension to the straps for that taut, urban cowboy look. For suits, you only need enough lift to bring your hips in an inch or two, thus allowing the outfit to drape one's frame as intended by the ever-so-slim designer.

I thought about adding optional padding for those slender folks who want a fuller, more well rounded appearance but I think that's already been invented. Besides, I don't think there's as big of a market for that item. Nope, as far as I can see, more of us need an anti-gravity device than an air bag in our pants.

I'm not quite ready to launch my enterprise yet. There have been a few minor problems during testing. My Cousin LouBerta, a beautiful, big woman, had her straps too tight when she plopped down in her rocker last week. Sadly, she broke both of her shoulders. The doctor said that she'll be fine when the body cast comes off in a few weeks. On the other hand, my sister doesn't shrug her shoulders anymore when I ask her a question. Once we work out the kinks, I'm going to make an infomercial and change the world!

Ten Habits of Effective Parents

We working parents try to be all things for all people, Of course, that's impossible, so we settle for just surviving each day until the kids go to bed.

After years of highly technical research (watching Leave It to Beaver and the Cosbys), I have developed a list of Ten Habits of Pretty Effective Working Parents. I truly believe that adopting these habits can add years to a fast paced life.

1. Be innovative. Step outside the box. When my son informed me at 8 AM that he needed a horseshoe for show and tell at 8:20 AM, I didn't panic. I went to my vanity, dug out a hairpin and quickly reshaped it into the world's tiniest horseshoe.

2. Have a sense of humor. Look on the bright side. Laugh when your child accidentally breaks that antique family heirloom. What's more valuable, the child or the possession?

Later, go into your bedroom and cry like a baby.

3. Make your family a priority. Everyone can't be a stay-at-home mom or dad. When you're with your family, give them your full attention. Forget the office and the committees for a little while. If you can't, just look at them intently as your mind drifts and say, "That's nice, sweetie" every few minutes.

4. Develop close personal friendships with at least two dependable stay-at-home moms or dads. It's even better if your kids attend the same school. It's one of Murphy's laws that children always get sick at school when you're 100 miles away. These people are angels and their job is much harder than yours. They will pick up your kids for you. They're usually at the school volunteering anyway, so it's not even out of their way. They also will come in handy for those wonderful birthday parties at 4 PM on Thursdays when the kids of working parents are in after-school care. Be sure to return the favor when you can, and always thank them profusely,

5. Remember your spouse. Your other half gets neglected sometimes as we attend to our life of details. Try to converse with them a little more than the national average of three minutes per day, Five minutes is pretty good.

6. Write things down. Forget the expensive day planner. Get a 49-cent spiral tablet and keep it in your purse. Put a big family calendar in the kitchen so you can moan about your lack of personal time weeks in advance.

7. Weird out. Do something totally out of the ordinary once in a while. It adds a little gaiety to the day. Put a temporary tattoo on your forearm on casual day at work. Wear hiking boots with your Anne Klein original. People will smile at you all day.

8. Be reliable. Say what you will do and do what you say in a timely manner. Return those calls, for goodness sakes! Be honest. I much prefer, "I'm sorry, but I'm overextended right now and I can't help with that project." to "Was that today?!"

9. Pamper yourself. Forget that mess about reserving an hour each day for introspection. Who has an entire hour free every day? If I have a free hour, I'm going to sleep-me and my inner child. If you happen to chance upon a free hour and a half, go ahead and exercise for 30 minutes or read a magazine. You might even talk to your spouse.

10. Never give up. Never say impossible. Fight that cold with home remedies until you get walking pneumonia. Help your second-grader with her graduate-level homework until midnight. Mail your Christmas cards out on Dec. 24. I filled out invitations to a birthday party while having my gallbladder removed.

By the way, you're all invited. It's Thursday, at four.

Loan Shark

I know that he doesn't like to be bothered when he's reading the paper but I was desperate. I stood there a moment hoping he'd notice me but he just kept reading. Finally, I said, "Excuse me, but could you please loan me $5?"

He lowered the paper a few inches and peered at me over the edge.

"What do you need the money for?" he asked suspiciously.

"I need gas. I'm running late for work already, and I don't have time to get money and gas."

"Can't you charge it?" he suggested. "That place down the street let's you pay at the pump."

Exasperated, I sighed loudly. I couldn't believe that my own flesh and blood was hedging about loaning me a measly five spot.

"I don't want to charge it. We're in enough debt. I'm still paying for that birthday dinner with all 20 of your very best friends." He was clearly unmoved by my financial problems. His eyes were straying back to the newspaper. If he started reading again, all hope was lost. If I could only find his wallet, I would just take the money and put it back before he noticed. He hides it so well that it would take a whole unit of police K9's to sniff it out.

"Come on," I plead. "I'll pay you back today, but I've got to get to work."

"With interest?"

"Son, I'm your mother for goodness sake! I gave you that money in the first place. How can you even think of charging me interest?"

An 8-year-old loan shark is a scary thing.

Funny, when it's HIS money being spent, he's a miser; but if it's MY money, the sky is the limit. When I'm paying for the movie, he prefers the evening show with a large popcorn, a large drink, and candy. When he's paying for the movie, we go to the matinee and he's "not hungry." When I'm buying the shoes, he wants the three-figure, cushioned insole, leather-upper, silk-lined name brands.

Otherwise, he wants to cut the heel and toe out of his old shoes and wear them as sandals. I love the idea of him being fiscally conservative, but I don't want him to become a Scrooge.

"Look, I am not paying you interest on a one day loan. Why don't I just charge you $2 for sleeping here last night? And let's tack on another 50 cents for the bath water. We'll be generous and give you the clothes for free but breakfast and transportation to school is $2.50. Those are bargain prices! So now you owe me five bucks. Give it up."

The look on his face was priceless.

"But Mom, you're supposed to do those things," he protested.

"Why?" I replied pointedly.

I could see the wheels spinning in his head as he slowly stood up and walked over to the stereo. He pried the cover off one of the speakers and retrieved his wallet from inside. As he handed me a crisp $20 bill, he said, "Okay, you can have the five dollars, but I still want my change."

I laughed and gave him a big hug, free of charge.

Albino Cow

A few months ago, before I became aware of Texas' "Veggie Libel Law," I said something unflattering about spinach. I am so sorry. I take it all back. If it's good enough for Popeye, it's good enough for me.

Now that we've cleared up that misunderstanding, I've just gotta tell you about our road trip to South Texas. We were headed to San Antonio when my husband saw a billboard advertising "The World's Only Albino Cow!" As the leading authority on State Fair freak shows, he felt compelled to witness this bovine anomaly. I agreed only because I desperately needed to use the restroom. Somehow we didn't have enough time when I suggested a quick stop at the Texas Ranger Museum in Waco, but we could stop for the cow.

Anyway, 20 minutes later, we're still looking for Brown's farm, home of the Albino Cow. We spotted a weathered cowboy retrieving his mail and stopped to ask for directions. My husband doesn't mind stopping for directions. I have to do the asking, but he'll stop and wait for me.

I rolled down the window and said, "Mister, can you please give me directions to Brown's farm?"

He smiled and said, "Sure can, darling. Head up the road another mile and hook a left at the big oak tree with the Michelin tire swing on it. Then a few yards beyond the pond with the three ducks in it, you take a right onto County Road Four. There used to be four ducks in that pond but Zeb's old three-legged dog ate the little ugly, gray duck last Christmas. But it was cold that day so Zeb didn't get too mad at him. Deke, that's Zeb's boy, got all riled up about it but he's fit to be tied most days 'cause he's thirty-years-old and still single. That poor boy's hands are bigger than his feet and he wears a size 17 Triple-E! No girl in her right mind is going to marry a man with big monkey hands like that–"

"Yessir, I'm sorry about Deke and the ugly duck, but how much farther is it to Brown's farm after we turn on County Road Four?"

"Oh, it's just a few yards more. You'll see Brown's big red barn as soon as you make the turn."

"That's great. We're going to see the Albino Cow."

"Y'all didn't fall for that trick did you?" he said laughing. "Them 4-H boys put that sign up as a prank. Every day some tourist comes through here looking for that cow. Old man Brown's got a goat with no ears and a chicken with lips, but he ain't got no white cows."

My husband looked so disappointed that the man invited us to dinner. "Y'all come on up to the house. The kids can ride our pony, and I'll grill you some steaks big as Deke's hands."

How can you turn down an offer like that?

Back on the highway with full stomachs and empty bladders, we sang show tunes and counted all the blue minivans we passed. We reached San Antonio just as night reclaimed the endless sky.

Our friends offered to take us out for dinner.

"No thanks," I declined, "We're stuffed. We had steaks as big as Deke's hands on the way down here."

"What?"

"Never mind. It's a long story. But next time you come our way, make sure you stop at Brown's farm outside of Temple and check out the Albino Cow."

Fender Bender

These are a few of my favorite sounds:

I like the gurgling sound of the ATM machine just before it graciously spits out money when I haven't balanced my checkbook in a while and I'm not sure if the mortgage check has cleared and I don't get paid for two days. I like the sound of my children giggling in the den as they watch Saturday morning cartoons. And who doesn't love the sound of the garage door slamming shut at the end of a long day, especially that day when I almost killed someone?

No, I'm not a violent person. I don't cause scenes in restaurants because no one has refilled my tea glass. Never do I throw tantrums in department stores because they won't let me return a sweater for cash without a receipt. I don't even yell at the rude drivers who tailgate and flash their lights to force me into another lane. Sure, I think really ugly things about them but I never move my lips, and I don't look at them as they pass me.

However, that particular day was doomed from the start. I was running late when I discovered that I had a flat tire. Then, my husband put that little toy tire on that they give you for a spare these days so everyone in the world will know that you ran over a nail. Then I had a long workday with a stressful committee meeting at lunch. I use the term lunch generically because I didn't get to eat anything. As twilight descended, I gratefully headed home in a light mist and heavy traffic.

That's when it happened. This huge Lincoln in front of me stopped abruptly to let the wind pass by, and I slid right into the back of it.

BANG!

Actually, it was more like, bang. We weren't going very fast, yet visions of traffic arguments that resulted in fatalities raced through my head as I watched the biggest woman that I'd ever seen in my life unfold from the driver's seat of this car. She slammed her door and glared at me. I quaked in my seat as she marched to the rear of her car. She looked at her bumper and she looked at mine. I was not getting out of my car so that woman could shake me like a rag doll.

As she made her way toward me with a scowl that would make Bob Dole look friendly, I suddenly remembered what was under my seat. I reached down and wrapped my fist around the cold piece of metal. She tapped on the window. I let it down a few inches and stammered, "I'm very sorry. I hope you're all right. I have insurance–"

"Wait a minute!" she barked.

I leaned back and brought my right hand up to my side. She couldn't see what I was holding in the dim light.

"Listen," she said, "everything is fine. No harm done. A squirrel ran in front of my car, and I didn't want to hit it. Sorry about that."

Whew, that was a close call. I was so glad that I hadn't made a hasty decision and done something I would have regretted. When I told my husband about the incident, he said, "What were you going to do with the radar detector?"

"Well, I thought that maybe I could throw it at her and distract her long enough for me to get out of the car and run like the wind. Maybe she would have collapsed trying to catch me."

He just shook his head and laughed along with me. I like that sound best of all.

The F-Word

I did it again. I failed Motherhood 101. I'm beginning to think that I will never get this parenting thing down pat.

Kids should come with an instruction manual. Everything in our home came with some sort of manual or guide. Even the sofa came with instructions and it just sits there. The hospital just handed us the kids along with a huge bill, and they're the most complicated things in the house.

Recently, Jay found me alone in the laundry room.

"Mom," he whispered, "Ray said a really bad word today."

"What word was that Jay?" I inquired, putting wet clothes into the dryer.

"He said the F-word when we were playing soccer a little while ago. You told us never to say the F-word," he lowered his head and looked sad as if to say, " I hate to do this but I'm just the messenger."

I was shocked. I never (well, rarely) use the F-word and never in front of the kids. I couldn't even remember discussing it with them. Perhaps we overheard it in some PG movie, and I told them to refrain from foul language. I just couldn't imagine my angel using that awful word.

I stormed into the den and confronted Ray.

"Young man," I yelled, "I better never hear filthy language coming from your mouth again!"

He stared at me in shock.

"You are setting a poor example for your brother and the other youngsters in the neighborhood. I am so disappointed in you. You go to your room right now and stay there until I tell you to come out. Now march!"

He looked at me all teary-eyed. "But Mom, what did I say?

"Jay told me you said the F-word several times today and you know how I feel about bad words."

"But all I said was Fart. Everyone was saying it. We farted every time we scored a goal. Dad says 'fart' sometimes."

I felt two inches tall. A puff of gas could have knocked me over at that moment. I tried to make it up to him the next day. During my lunch break, I went to the toy store and bought the very expensive Super Soaker 4000 for his best friend's birthday party that weekend. It's a water gun that holds about eight gallons of water and shoots a jet stream for a hundred yards. I even had it gift-wrapped and bought a matching card. When I got home, I told him what I'd done.

"Mom, nobody likes that one anymore," he said. "Now, everybody likes the Super Soaker 5000. Carson shot his brother in the eye with one, and now he wears a patch over the hole where his eye used to be. It's way cool."

"What about the card? Is it OK?" I asked, desperate for approval. "See, it has that cartoon character Doug on it. You watch Doug every day right?"

"Doug is dumb. I only watch him because Bart Simpson comes on next. Nobody likes Doug."

"Well, what am I suppose to do with this gift?

"I guess I'll take it. We can give my friend some money instead."

Oh friggle, fraggle!

Third Grade Homework

I'm having a hard time with the third grade. I did pretty well in it the first time around back in nineteen– well, many years ago. But this time around, I don't know if I'll pass. Actually it's my youngest boy, Arthur, that's in the third grade. It feels like we're both going through this class though. Only nine more years of homework, and then he's on his own.

School has changed so much in the years since I wore pigtails and sneakers. Arthur has a computer class. To him a computer is more than a typewriter with a television screen. I taught myself every thing I know about computers, which is practically nothing. For years, I thought a hard drive was rush hour traffic on a rainy day.

Math I can handle pretty well. They've adopted some different terminology but one and one is still two, at least for now.

Arthur really likes Mrs. Matheson's class. He talks about her all the time.

Yesterday, he told me, "Mrs. Matheson is really nice. She says I'm a good student."

"That's great son," I replied. "Which class does she teach?" He has several teachers, and I get them mixed up sometimes.

"I don't know," he said, "but we have it everyday before lunch."

"Well what do you talk about in this class?"

He thought a moment and said, "People."

Each night we go over his homework. "Arthur, " I explained as we sat at the kitchen table reviewing for a test, "A culture is a way of life."

"A culture is a way of life," he repeated confidently.

"And the most important crop grown in the Americas was corn."

After that revelation, things started to get a little complicated. I continued to read aloud, "Clovis points made hunting easier."

"What are Clovis points?" he wondered.

"Something you use for hunting I guess."

Brilliant answer, I know. I glanced over the rest of the test questions and got a little nervous. I never knew that the Anasazi held their religious services in a kiva. That seemed a little advanced for an eight-year-old.

"When is this test, son?" I asked anxiously. He hadn't filled in his name or the test date at the top of the paper.

He couldn't remember anything. He couldn't remember which class the test was in or which teacher had given him the paper. How in the world was he going to remember that the Mayas developed their civilization by borrowing on the ideas of the Olmecs? Maybe I am underestimating him, I thought. So we plowed ahead with our studies.

We had been sitting there for an hour with an encyclopedia and three dictionaries when my fifth grader came into the kitchen to get something to drink. He looked at us with a puzzled expression and said, "What are ya'll doing with my homework? I've been looking everywhere for that paper."

His little brother heaved a big sigh of relief and said, "Thank goodness! This stuff is making me die."

Maybe we'll make it through third grade, after all.

You're Embarrassing Me

One sunny afternoon, I was sitting in the park eating my lunch of a peanut butter and syrup sandwich with a diet Coke when I saw a cute little family of ducks. The mother duck was leading her four little ducklings across a large field of bluebonnets toward the pond on the east side of the park. As she neared the water, one little duck fell behind. He appeared to be watching the children swinging, although it's rather difficult to tell what a duck is thinking. Most of the time, the ducks I'm around have orange sauce on them and they're not thinking anything anymore.

Anyway, the mother duck glanced back at the little straggler and in a clearly annoyed voice she said, "Quack, quack, quack!" I interpreted that to mean, "Child, will you please come on! Don't you know those crazy human children like to chase ducks? Hurry up before they see you!"

The little duck sped up a bit, but he didn't seem to be in a great big rush. In exasperation, his mother finally waddled over to him and swatted him across the head with her orange beak. He actually blushed. I never knew ducks could blush, did you? Really, he hung his little head, and his cheeks turned crimson.

As he waded into the pond, he looked at his mother and made the most pathetic little "quack" sound I've ever heard. I'm not Dr. Doolittle but I could swear he said, "Mom, you're embarrassing me."

My kids came out of the womb saying that. Apparently, I am the most outrageous, eccentric, downright weirdest woman on the planet. Everything I do embarrasses my kids. If I try to kiss them in front of their friends, I embarrass them. If I drive them to school in my housecoat, I embarrass them. If I climb the fence at the football field because I don't want to walk all the way to the gate, I have to hear about it.

"Mom, don't do that. None of the other moms climb over the fence like that."

I try to explain: "Son, the other moms can't climb a fence, you should be proud of me."

But they're not proud - they're embarrassed. I do believe that it is my sworn duty as a mother to embarrass my children. It's an American tradition. It's a family tradition. My mother embarrassed me every time we had open house at school.

She intentionally developed a huge cold sore on her upper lip three times a year just so she could gross out all of my teachers. Sometimes she tried to cover it with pancake makeup that only made it look more hideous. My grades dropped during the two weeks after Open House. The teachers were punishing me for my mother's indecent exposure.

My mother says that her mother embarrassed her. My grand-mother says her mother embarrassed her, and so on and so on. Who am I to break with tradition? Some day, children, you'll get to embarrass your kids.

Frankly, it's kind of fun.

You Look Nice Dear

I have been happily married for many years. Now, I use that phrase lightly because there were several days in there, which probably add up to a few months, where I was not too thrilled with my other half. And vice versa, of course, if you must know. So let's just say that I've been pretty content with this matrimony thing for a good while.

I've noticed that the years have brought dramatic changes in the way that Honey Bunny and I treat each other. For one thing, I don't call him Honey Bunny as often. I now call him "Did" as in, "Did, you eat all of the ice cream?" and "Did you remember to go by the dry cleaners?"

He fondly refers to me as "Where" as in "Where, are my car keys?" or "Where, is the remote?" Surely this is our way of saying, "You are important to me, darling. I couldn't bear to live without you." We still have a lot of fun whenever we manage to get together. Lately, though, we've been taking each other a little for granted. I suppose this happens with all married couples as their lives start to revolve around kids and careers.

The first year of our marriage, I ironed his ties and read all these books on how to please a man. (They were all written by single women, of course.) He seemed to enjoy the results, but after a while I noticed that all he ever read were sports magazines and the newspaper. I burned those books and went back to reading trashy romance novels.

Recently he informed me that it would be nice if I started wearing attractive lingerie again instead of his old T-shirts and flannel pajamas. Yuk! I hate that stuff. It's cold, and it scratches. And he certainly doesn't wear anything attractive to bed. He wears jogging shorts, for goodness sakes! He has a hundred-year-old set of cotton pajamas that he wears when my folks come to visit but that hardly counts.

So I tried to compromise, for his sake. I would be sexy but warm. I cut the arms and legs off of my blue-and-green plaid flannel pajamas and sewed them onto a red teddy. He wasn't exactly pleased. I even threw on a pair of silver pumps to complete the ensemble. He slept in the guestroom that night. Some people have no sense of humor.

He does give me compliments. He just says the same thing every time: "You look very nice, dear." I could shave my head and pierce my eyelid, and he'd say, "You look very nice, dear." I could put on a shrink-to-fit $25,000 Bob Mackie evening gown and he'd say, "You look very nice, dear."

That's what you say to women that are 10 months pregnant:

"No, Marsha, you don't look like an elephant in that mini skirt. You look very nice, dear."

Come on! Fifteen years of the same compliment. I want some creativity, some enthusiasm. Say it with feeling!

Once, I visited my sister at the University of Oklahoma, and she introduced me to some of her male classmates. As we walked away, one of the young men exclaimed, "Dang old girl is fine!" (Forget the old part.) I was so excited! I floated all the way back to Texas, where I told everyone who would listen that a 20-year-old collegian thought I was fine!

Yeah, that's what I'm talking about. That's a compliment. Those worthless magazine articles about walking two steps behind your husband and cleaning the toilet with a smile on your face also said that you should treat your husband like you want to be treated. So as we were driving to church on Sunday, I said, "Honey, you look like a fashion model in that suit. I'm proud to be your escort."

He grinned from ear to ear, patted my hand and replied, "Thank you, dear, and you look really nice, too."

The Other Woman in Red

She was the other woman in his life. The woman in red. She always wore that scintillating shade, like a State Fair candy apple. A head turning, sleek, curvaceous kind of crimson. I've heard that the eye sees red first and that's why warning lights and stop signs are always red. It's a color designed to capture your attention. It certainly snared my man.

I was no match for that girl. She willingly prowled the streets late into the night, laughing at my fear of the things that go bump in the night. The lady was smooth like an aged brandy. I don't ever drink brandy because it smells like lighter fluid and the fumes make my eyes water so I don't really know if it's smooth or not. Let's just say that she was smooth like ice cream, Blue Bell ice cream. Incredibly smooth, with no fat.

Who could blame him for choosing her over a simpleton like me? I hated his loud music but she rocked to the beat until his cassette deck started smoking and the Temptations began to sound like Barry Manilow.

Yeah, she was easy to please. So many times I watched them from behind the curtain of my bedroom window. I hated all the time he spent by her side and the way he looked at her as if she was a priceless work of art. I was jealous of the praise he showered on her to impress his friends. He didn't even try to hide his love, his indiscretion. Whenever I confronted him, he always said, "Baby, it's just a car. You know I love you more than my car."

Maybe he did love me more but not much more. That was his first car. He was 18, I was 17, and the car was 10-years-old. It was a very used two-door Chevrolet Astra with bald tires and more mileage than Air Force One. He spent a fortune on Q-tips and Armor All to groom his little baby. He washed that car so much that the windshield wrinkled up like a prune.

There's just something magical about that first car and whether it's new or used doesn't even matter. It's your car, your very own. That elation lasts for days or weeks until some dufus puts a dent in the door or a scratch on the bumper like the time Cola Lola stepped on my new suede shoes that had been in layaway for two months and she ruined them. Boy, was I mad at her.

Anyway, I got into my husband's truck this morning and goodness, have times changed. I had to dig through the trash on the floor to find the accelerator. When I started the vehicle, three warning lights came on. I'm sure his truck used to be green but it's a dusty brown these days. He washes it once a month if he has a coupon. I overheard him telling his friend that he's tired of her and he's going to trade her in for a new model.

I assume he was talking about his truck. As I kissed him goodbye and wished him a good day, he noticed my new fragrance.

"Hmmm, I like that perfume," he said. "Is that new? What is it called?"

I smiled coyly as he surveyed my shiny arms and legs.
"It's Eau de Armor All," I said.

Hey, I've got a few miles myself, you know.

Dinner Guests

Four steaks. Nice cuts. Seasoned, sizzling ribeyes.

Four plates. Everyday ware. Two are slightly chipped but that's OK.

Four forks and four knives.

Four glasses filled with ice and Hi C.

One question.

"Mom, can Petey stay for dinner?"

Petey. Where did Petey come from? I didn't hear the doorbell. How long has he been here? Why hasn't Petey eaten already? It's 8 PM for goodness sakes. If I hadn't worked late, we would have eaten at 7:45, after my nap.

Of course, I keep these thoughts in my mind and say what any good mother would say.

"Is Petey hungry?" I ask, hoping that he's already filled his little tummy with pop and candy.

I'm not against sharing the wealth but I only have FOUR steaks for my family of FOUR. If we were having spaghetti or hot dogs, no problem. But steak night is rare and sacred. I am not giving up my steak, not even for sweet little Petey.

My son checks the status of Petey's appetite and tells me, "He's says he's starving, Mom. He hasn't eaten since lunch at school today."

Oh good grief. He's starving! Why does he have to be starving? If he was just hungry, I could make him a bologna sandwich and send him home to dinner but no, he's starving! Here's my chance to help with world hunger and it has to happen on steak night.

I try another tactic.

"Tell him to call home and check with his Mom. She's probably wondering where he is this late on a school night," I suggest.

I'll even give him a ride home because it's dark outside. That's a decent gesture, right?

By now, everyone, both my sons and Petey, is in the kitchen with me.

Petey says, "My parents had to go to a meeting. No one is home but my sister. Do you want me to call her?"

No, she might be hungry too, I think to myself.

"That's all right," I tell him. "You guys go and wash your hands while I set another place at the table.

Four steaks, each cut in half, makes a platter of meat. We pass the platter around the table. My husband takes one of the pieces and each of my sons take one semicircle of beef. I am so proud of them.

Petey just looks for a long time and then he takes the smallest piece.

"Petey, I thought you were starving," I say. "Don't you want another piece of meat? You can have two."

My boys, who count slices of pizza like they're $20 bills, stare at me incredulously. I look back at them with an expression that says, he's your starving friend, I'm just trying to be nice

Petey declines my offer so everyone else immediately takes another slice, leaving one lonely piece for my dining pleasure. Petey smiles at me, his braces glistening with Hi-C.

After dinner, I pardon the boys from their dishwashing duties and tell them to escort Petey back to his residence. There wasn't much to wash. All the plates were clean except Petey's. He left two green beans and half of his half of a steak.

I looked around for witnesses and then I do what any good mother would do.

Guess.

Hey, I'm not throwing steak in the trash. Not even sweet, little Petey's steak.

Mom, Don't Come

I know the difference between a hat trick and a field goal. I know the difference between a nine-iron and a sand wedge - even though I'm terrible with a sand wedge. This spring, I used one to dig holes for my flowerbed. I just put a practice ball on the spot where I wanted to plant the bulb and pretended I was in a sand trap. I never did hit that ball but my tulips were gorgeous. And, yes, I know the difference between a Mustang and a Corvette. These are simple matters.

But what is the difference between, "Mom, you don't have to come," and "Mom, you don't need to come."

Ouch! That still hurts. Give me a moment please– OK, I'll be all right in a second. I really don't believe that my son meant to bruise my feelings. He's a sweet man-boy. And frankly, the singular idea of spending another two hours of my life on the sideline of some mom-forsaken field as fire rains from the sky is not appealing. It never was really.

I've done it time after time, field after field, bleacher after bleacher, for years, however. I've lugged the coolers, yelled out encouragement for the wrong mascot, and purchased thousands of losing raffle tickets. And why have I been such a devoted, rabid fan for so many teams? Why? Because of my son. Where he went, I went.

Sure, I sat on the practice sidelines balancing my checkbook, making phone calls, and reading novels. Yes, I've spent the entire half time of soccer games in the women's restroom trying to escape the merciless heat or Arctic cold. But when the team was in motion, whenever my son moved, even if he was just scratching himself, I saw it. It was recorded in my mind for all time. I battled entire battalions of mosquitoes for my boy just because he asked, "Mom, you're coming to my game aren't you?"

He said it like a sentence though, like he expected me there because he wanted me there. He needed me. So, as often as I could, through headaches and heartaches, I went to his games.

Now, suddenly, he says, "Mom, you don't need to come to practice anymore." To soften the blow, he added; none of the other moms come. Oh, so now it's a Dad thing. Dad can come but I'm not welcome.

I'm cool. I don't wear goofy clothes or yell, "Hit him again!" at basketball games. I don't run on the field and do cart wheels with the cheerleaders - anymore. What happened? Why was I banished?

I think it's this awful robber that keeps coming to our home at night. I used to call him the man fairy, but fairies are nice people. They bring you cute little things like tooth money and tiaras. This guy is a thief. First he took my son's fat, baby cheeks away. Then he stole his giggles and hugs. This summer he ferreted away his little boy voice and left a voice box that rumbles like thunder and sounds like my husband. Those things I expected. I was sort of prepared for those losses.

But I never dreamed he'd steal my son's desire for my company. Gee. That's been the hardest loss of all.

But I'm fighting back. The thief can have my baby's adolescence. The girls can even have his attention, but his friendship, our friendship, is priceless. No one is taking our relationship away without going through me first and I just ain't having it! Not today, not tomorrow, not ever.

Last Saturday, I went to practice anyway. There were several moms there. I think my son even looked my way once, and smiled, during practice. He didn't complain but he did say, "Mom, when you come to practice again, will you bring me some Gatorade?"

Ultimately, I suppose, the difference between us depends a lot on me.

See you at practice.

New Woman

I've decided that my husband needs a new woman. We've been married a long time and as incredible as it seems, I believe he's getting a little bored with me. Granted, I've been telling the same corny jokes for the past ten years, but those are the only ones that I can remember. I can never remember the really good jokes that make me laugh from way down in my tummy for more than a couple of days.

Anyway, I was reading one of those women's magazines and it said that men need a little excitement, something spicy and different, to keep their interest. The article didn't mention what men need to do in order to keep their women interested, but I guess that's not a hot topic. I thought I'd save Honey Bunny the trouble of having to hunt for an exciting new woman by just finding someone suitable myself.

I looked everywhere, high and low, up and down, hither and yon. I could not find a single, half way decent woman anywhere in our backyard. I gave up my exhaustive search and turned instead to my mirror.

I can be different, spicy and exciting, I thought. All I need is a good wig, some bronze lipstick, a pair of spiked heels and a little duct tape. It took me two weeks and a home equity loan to acquire everything I needed to make the transformation. (I needed a lot of duct tape.)

You should have seen my man's face when he arrived home Friday evening. I greeted him wearing: a long, shimmering gown, the high heels, false eyelashes, and a wonderful wig that I purchased from a home shopping infomercial.

He dropped his briefcase and his jaw onto the floor, then he said, "Don't tell me you're going to be a bridesmaid again. Who's getting married this time?"

"No one is getting married. This isn't a bridesmaid's dress. OK, I did wear it in a wedding last year but I took the bows off and cut a split up the side. Don't I look spicy and exciting?"

"Sure, you look great, but why do you have that cane? Are you injured?"

"No, I can't walk in these shoes. The heels are too high."

"Well let me help you to a chair. You probably can't see either with all that hair in your face. Is that a wig?"

"No, I just pulled on my ponytail real hard and my hair grew twelve inches. Of course, it's a wig, silly. Don't you like it?"

He tilted his head and examined me closely. "Are you sure you have it on the right way? There's something odd about the way it fits."

"Oh that's because it's a reversible wig. Actually, it's five looks in one. If I put the tag in the back like this, I look like Gloria Estefan. If I place the tag on the right, I'm Diana Ross. If I put it here, it's the Connie Chung look and when I turn it 180 degrees, I'm Dr. Ruth. But wait, there's more, check this out! I can flip it inside-out and I'm Isaac Hayes!"

"Isaac Hayes is a bald, male, rhythm and blues singer."

"I know. I thought maybe you could wear it for me sometimes."

He laughed uneasily like he was trying to humor me. It was kind of like the way he laughs at those old jokes of mine. My shoulders slumped wearily as I conceded defeat. It seemed that I had failed to move his excitement meter one iota.

"Don't you like my new look?" I queried. "I wanted to be exciting and mysterious for you."

"I didn't have a problem with the old look," he said. "Excitement and mystery are highly overrated. Actually, I'm OK if you're OK. OK?"

"Oh, thank goodness," I said relieved. "Now get some scissors and help me with this duct tape. I think I've lost circulation in my legs."

On Hold

I'm on hold. It's not the warm embrace kind of "hold me, hold me, hold me." It's the "Thank you, for your patience. Someone will be with you before the next millennium," kind of hold. I can't hang up. I've invested too much time into this call. If I hang up, I'll lose my place in the infinitely long line of people waiting to speak to a human being, any human being, at this company.

Thank goodness, for cellular phones. I've been able to purchase groceries, fill my car up with gas, cook a four-course meal (milk counts as a course), and clean up the kitchen while waiting for a customer service representative. My four-hour battery will need charging again real soon but hopefully, I'll reach a live one before then.

It all started innocently enough. While reviewing my credit card statement, I found an item that I had a question about. A simple question. So I dialed the toll-free service number under the illusion that I could resolve the matter in a few minutes. Instead I got this.

"Thank you for calling Bank of Eternity, for faster service please have your account number available."

OK, got it right here. No problem.

"For account information or service, press 1. To apply for a new account, press 2. To hear an oral reading of Volumes 1 and 2 of the Encyclopedia Britannica while you wait, press 3."

Well, that's a nice attempt at humor, I thought. Little did I realize they were serious. So I pressed number 1.

Then I heard, "Please enter your twenty digit account number followed by the pound key within the next ten seconds."

It took me five attempts to accomplish that feat within the time limit. I was disconnected twice in the meantime. After that, I received more instructions.

"Please enter the last two digits of your mother's weight on her eighteenth birthday, followed by the pound key."

I clicked over, called my Mom, verified the information, hung up with Mom, and entered the two digits. I kept thinking that at any moment they were going to ask me to pull a sword from a stone and slay a dragon to prove that I actually deserved to speak to a customer service representative.

Finally, there appeared a light at the end of the tunnel when I heard the automated voice say, "Please hold while we connect you to your account representative."

Two days later, I finally heard a real voice.

"Thank you for waiting," she said. "This is Tammy. May I have your account number please?"

"But Tammy, I just entered my account number five times. Didn't your computer save it or something?"

Tammy sighed. "Well, ma'am our computers have been down most of the day, so that information didn't transfer. May I please have your account number, your telephone number, and your home address?"

"But Tammy when I applied for the card. I gave a deposition on everything there is to know about me. I even sent you a vial of blood with the fourteen copies of my birth certificate. Isn't that account number linked to my account information?"

"Ma'am, I just work here. There are two of us left since they downsized the department. We share a single computer and it's ten-years-old. Jean takes care of twenty-five states and I handle the others. I'm sure all of your information is in the computer somewhere but I could carve it in stone faster than I can pull it up."

Fine. I gave her all of my information again and waited some more while she went to lunch. When she came back from lunch, she asked me, "What was your question again, ma'am?"

By now, I could hardly remember my question.

"Well, there's a thirty dollar charge on my card for some kind of phone or Internet service. I've never heard of this company and my husband says that he doesn't know what it is either. Can you tell me anything about these charges?

"Ma'am, you'll have to call the company for that information."

"What company is it? All I have here are some initials."

"I understand ma'am. I'd like to help you but unfortunately, I just noticed that you live in Texas."

"And?"

"Ma'am, that's Jean's area. I'll have to transfer you. Please hold."

Padre Island

Dear children,

With much sadness and an overwhelming desire to be washing laundry, I am writing you from the entirely too sunny beaches of South Padre Island. Reluctantly, I am spending a few days of vacation here with your godmother. Oh, how she begged and pleaded for me to come!

I have spent most of the past two days alone while she attends meetings with other attorneys from all over Texas. Contrary to what I told you before I left, I have not been forced to attend those meetings with her. She did tell me that the meeting room is cold. That made me sad.

Furthermore, there have been no hurricanes or floods as I predicted. I guess it's not the rainy season, after all. Happily, neither the placid Laguna Madre on the west or the Gulf of Mexico on the east is filled with tar and dead fish.

Actually, the entire 34 miles of beaches, nature trails and wildlife preserves are quite lovely. As soon as we crossed the 2.5-mile-long Queen Isabella Causeway upon our arrival, I knew that I misled you guys. So sorry.

I just wanted you to know, oh, what was I going to say? That room service lady interrupted my thoughts. Hmmm, this coffee is good! Well, I'm only eating a bagel since it's almost lunchtime. Seems I overslept again.

Meanwhile, I'll just lie out on that hot beach in my jeans and afghan again while the sailboats drift by. I wanted to stay in my room, make the bed, and scrub the toilets like I do at home, but the maid insisted that I leave and allow her to do her job. Oh well. Since there is no TV in my room that I've noticed and the phone never rings, I guess it's OK to trudge across that hot sand out to the cool water's edge. So, so boring. I don't know if you'd like it here at all.

Except for the waves meandering into the blue sky at the horizon, nothing exciting is happening. For the sake of your godmother, however, I'll pretend to be relaxing and enjoying this trip.

I miss you terribly. Can't wait to come home. Take care of Dad, and, yes, I'm bringing you something extremely cool back.

All my love,

Mom

P.S. Remember to brush your teeth and hair.

Algebra Test

Whew! I'm exhausted. Going back to school was one of the worst decisions I've ever made, and I've made some pretty bad ones over the years.

I've been up late several nights studying and reviewing for a big test. I think the results count for a third of my final grade. What was I thinking to enroll in such a difficult course after all these years out of school?

It was so much easier when I was younger and permanently in that "student mode." Studying and taking tests wasn't such a big deal. But now I've got so many other responsibilities between my family and my full-time job that I'm having trouble keeping up with the younger and obviously smarter kids in this class.

I probably wouldn't be stressing about this so much if it weren't for the fact that I've already taken this course. That was many years ago and I made a passing grade as I recall. Sadly, I've forgotten almost everything I learned.

I suppose I should clarify that it's actually my son taking pre-algebra, not me. But it sure feels like I'm taking it, too. Frankly, I'm not that good at algebra. My husband and I pulled straws to see who would help Junior and according to my spouse, I won.

It's just too bad that "x" and "y" and I do not get along. They have too many psychological issues. What is "x"? What is the function of "y"?

I don't know. I've got my own problems. I don't have time to help x and y find their inner child. I don't know what my purpose is on this planet let alone the future of these two confused letters.

Don't get me wrong. I love to help my kiddos with their home-work. It's quality time and I get to see how their little minds are developing. Critical thinking skills are very important. If I discover a weak area, we work on it together until they grasp the concept. But what happens when you get to the parents' weak areas? I'm not going to ever admit to my kid that he is now smarter than I am.

He may soon come to that realization on his own, but he'll never hear it from me.

One night I pondered so long over a problem that he finally asked me, "Are you sure you know what you're doing? I can call Brandon if I need to, his mom is really good at math."

"Son, I know what I'm doing. I've been helping you all these years and you've done fine, right?"

"Yeah, but I missed some problems on that last assignment that you helped me with."

"I only helped you with two questions."

"Those were the only two that I missed."

Well excuse me, but in my world, two negatives do not equal a positive. Two negatives equal a pink slip and a tight budget.

I was so worried about that exam that I couldn't sleep. Finally, around 2 AM, I got up to check on Junior who, of course, was under the haystack fast asleep. I don't know how much longer I can hold out before we have to call Brandon's mom. That's like having another woman in my kitchen, using my pots and cooking for my family.

On second thought, that doesn't sound too bad, actually. If you'll kindly excuse me, I need to make a quick call. We've still got a semester and a half to go.

Tattling

Would someone from Tattler's Anonymous please call and let me know the time and place of your next meeting? I need to enroll my baby boy into your 14-step program. [I know it usually only takes 12 steps but he's got it bad.]

He doesn't know the meaning of the word "closed-mouthed." He doesn't know the meaning of the word "discretion." He doesn't know the meaning of "privileged information." In fact, he doesn't know the meaning of a lot of words because he's just a kid. However, I truly wish that he'd stop taking his self-appointed role as the thorn in his big brother's side so seriously. This kid has a talent for telling.

Before he learned his ABC's, he had memorized my work number, my cell phone number, my pager number, and my fax number. He could track me down better than a Dixie blood hound.

As time passed, the novelty of his Junior Central Intelligence Agency wore off and I told him to stop calling me every time his brother forgets to cover his mouth when he coughs. That's when he started sending faxes to my office. The latest one was a typical report on the subversive activity going on in my home.

To: Monica Anderson [Mom]

From: Jacob Anderson

No. of Pages: 2 [Including cover]

Message: My brother has been using the same face towel for three weeks. I think that is why he has those little bumps on his nose and forehead. Please call home and punish him. Maybe you should give his new basketball to me.

Yours very truly,

The Good Son

I hate to cut him off completely for fear that he'll have some really juicy information eventually. On the other hand, if this thing starts spreading, soon my husband will know what really happened to that box of delicious, hot Krispy Kreme donuts.

Yes, I guess that settles it.

You T.A. folks give me a call. If you need my phone number, just check with my son. He'll tell you anything you want to know.

Jump, Bubba, Jump

"Jump! Bubba, Jump!"

I heard those three ominous words just seconds before the loud crash and the wet splash catapulted me from my comfortable chair. I went racing down the hall as Bubba's screams slid across the bathroom tile like a wet bar of soap. As I reached for the knob on the door to the bathroom, my oldest son tried to reassure his baby brother.

"Shh! Don't cry Bubba. I'll help you."

When I barreled through the bathroom door, they both gasped. Their eyes were as big as four silver-dollar pancakes next to a side of bacon and two freshly scrambled eggs at three in the morning when the new guy is working in the kitchen. That's pretty big.

I stood there huffing and puffing, which is pretty pathetic because I was only 20 yards away in the first place. I was thinking that I really do need to start exercising more often when I noticed that Bubba was stuck in the toilet. I found that strange even for Bubba who once put a grape up his nose simply because it fit.

He was squatting in the toilet bowl with his knees next to his little chest. The large towel pinned to his shirt like Superman's cape dangled over the seat. His right hand was grasping the bottom edge of the shower curtain that had fallen on top of his brother like a plastic blanket. The floor was covered with water.

Being an experienced mother, I didn't bother asking, "What happened in here?" The clues told it all. The little yellow rubber duck and the small gray shark that came with the cheeseburger were on the floor next to my husband's favorite fishing pole. Junior was sprawled across the bathtub trying to remove the shower curtain from his head. Every light in their room was burning despite the beautiful sunshine that had been provided by nature for free. That had nothing to do with their dilemma but it irritates the heck out of me.

Anyway, after quickly surveying the damage, I knew most of the story.

"Boys, let me just guess what happened here. Junior you thought it would be fun to go fishing in the toilet even though you got in trouble for going fishing in the bathtub last week. You were trolling for Great White sharks when this poor little innocent duckling drifted into the dangerous blue waters of the toilet bowl."

As I spoke, the boys were mesmerized by my psychic abilities. I could just hear their little minds asking, "How on earth does she do that?"

I pried Bubba from his porcelain prison as I pieced the clues together a la Sherlock Holmes.

"Because you are such brave and heroic lads, you knew that you had to do something to save the little duck before the evil shark swallowed him whole. So you pinned two of Mommy's best towels to your shirts because every super hero has to have a cape. Then you climbed onto the side of the bathtub where Junior convinced Bubba to grab the shower curtain, swoop down over the toilet, grab the little duck, and save the day only, Bubba landed in the water. The shower curtain rod fell, and Junior was knocked into the tub."

I repaired the damage, changed Bubba's clothes, and admonished them, "Please don't ever do this again. It's very dangerous. Besides I don't normally mop on Tuesdays."

As I left their room, I heard Junior whisper to Bubba, "Do you think she knows about the snake, too?

Tooth Fairy

I need your help. I'm issuing an all-points-bulletin for a missing person. I've known her for years, and she's very special to me. She's been to my home many, many times, but unfortunately, I don't have a picture of her. Actually, I can't even give you a very good description because I've never seen her face to face.

Here's what I do know about this dear lady. One, she's very, very fast. I'm talking track-star, world-class sprinter speed. And I think she's American, but it's hard to say. My friend is very generous. She's a bit of a night owl; she sleeps all day. She's quite the social butterfly and children adore her. She's petite in stature. I guess that's why she wears high heels with those long, formal gowns and the crystal tiara.

She's never been married. It's hard to meet a nice guy when you work at night. Let's see, she's very strong because she has to lift stuff and haul it around all the time. And she's loaded, big bucks! That's all that I can tell you except that she has a most unusual means of transportation. According to published reports, she doesn't have a car. Instead, she has wings!

Has anyone seen the tooth fairy?

I need to get in touch with her. The last two times that she was supposed to come by our house, she was a no-show.

My son is quite upset about it. A few days ago, he came barreling into my bedroom, clutching a little baby tooth in his fist. "Mom, " he whined, "the tooth fairy forgot to come again!"

Well shame on her. My husband glared at me from his pillow and shook his head disapprovingly. Now, why is this my fault? I don't even know how to contact this woman. She's been pretty reliable up until recently. Almost without fail, she shows up in the middle of the night, exchanges the tooth for money, and leaves without a peep.

Listen, I arrange all the doctor's visits, schedule the repair people and plan the vacations. Why must I be in charge of the fairy visits too?

I gave my son a reassuring hug and said, "Maybe she left the money in Mommy's wallet again. She does that when she's in a big rush."

We checked my purse but there was only a quarter and two pennies in there. Dad's wallet was as barren as a desert. I called 911 and learned that the tooth fairy is at home recovering from some minor surgery. It seems that she takes the baby teeth and gives them to elderly people who don't have any teeth. I told you she's nice. Well, while she was trying to deliver the teeth to some needy grandma, she dropped the heavy bag of teeth and fractured her big toe. Don't worry, she'll be fine.

Anyway, if you see her, please tell her to contact me. I had to write my son a check! I want my two dollars back.

Treats After The Game

There's a certain charm about little people playing sports that, for me, is regrettably absent in their older counterparts.

It's Fall and we're in the middle of football season. I can't help but notice how competitive my son, Dante, has become. Now it's "play to win" and "no pain no gain." That's OK but I really liked it so much better when he would run up to me after a game, all smiles and bright eyes, and say, "Mommie, did we win?"

"Son, you're always a winner," I'd respond with an enthusiastic hug and kiss.

My husband would just shake his head in disbelief.

So what if the team lost the soccer game by seven goals? If the boy didn't know, and I didn't care, why sweat the small stuff?

Then my son would say, "Where are the treats? Do they have Gummy Bears? I love soccer!"

"Honey, first you have to go huddle with the coach. Then you can have a treat."

"What's a huddle?"

"It's when a bunch of guys stand around in a circle and perspire while the coach talks and the parents look at their watches."

"Why do they do that?"

"I have no idea."

"What do the coaches say, Mommy?"

"Nothing that can't wait until the next practice, but it's tradition, Sweetie so run along now."

Fast forward eight years and the gridiron becomes a battlefield of mighty warriors. The young men swagger after a bone-crushing tackle and dance after a field goal. Opposing teams scout their opponents and insist on seeing the birth certificates of the blue-chip players.

The sandbox has become a minefield.

Tempers explode; the less talented players ride the pine. Coaches sprout pulsating veins in their necks. It's prime time; it's sixth-grade football.

After the game, my son is devastated. We barely won the game.

"Mom, did you see that? We stink. The line wasn't blocking. The secondary got burned. Man, we gotta practice more."

"Son, it was a great game. Some mistakes were made, but we won and I'm sure everyone did their best."

"Are you kidding? That's the worst game we've ever played, and besides you weren't even watching. I saw you. You spent the whole time talking to the other moms."

"That's not true son. You had 10 carries for ninety-seven yards. You would have gone over a hundred if we hadn't gotten those penalties. In the first quarter, you made three tackles and intercepted a poorly thrown pass intended for the tight end. In the second quarter, you tied your shoe three times and had a 40-yard punt. At half time, you sat on your helmet by your best friend, Elk. You fumbled twice in the third quarter, speaking of mistakes; but you recovered nicely and scored a touchdown on fourth and 15 behind some fine blocking by the right guard and tackle. And the last quarter was ho-hum but I did notice when that awful lineman scratched your hand and drew blood. I need to speak to his mother, by the way."

"I guess you we're paying attention."

"Of course, I love coming to your games. It's what I live for. Now, go on over to the huddle. The coach might be saying something important."

"But it's only Dad."

"I know, but go on over anyway."

"Did anyone bring treats?"

"I have some Gummy Bears in the car."

"Thanks, Mom. Football is great!"

"Yeah, I know," I reply.

As he walks away, I smile and glance at my watch.

Tupac the Turtle

We've had houseguests for two weeks exactly. The nicest thing I can say about them is that they're clean. Otherwise, they have many faults. They make noise all night long. Their special diets are driving me crazy and they won't communicate with us. My children talk to them constantly and they respond with only a nod or a glossy-eyed wink. I don't even like their names, Tupac and Madman. But I didn't have much of a choice because it was either them or a dog. I thought the turtles would be cheaper. Wrong again.

It seemed like a simple request.

"Mom, since we can't have a tiger, or an elephant, or a dog, or a cat, or a rattlesnake 'cause you're allergic to them, can we have a turtle?"

After a dozen emotional goldfish funerals, I felt guilty enough to buy the turtles.

"OK boys, if they're not too expensive, and you promise to take good care of them. I'll get you a turtle."

So off we went to the pet store in search of satisfaction. The box turtles were around $20. I figured we'd throw in a $10 aquarium, a little food, maybe a turtle toy or two, and I'd have enough money left over for one of Mrs. Fields' cookies and a drink.

Then the madness began. The boys almost came to blows trying to decide whether or not to get a box turtle, which prefers land, or a red-eared slider turtle that lives in the water. My money was on the box turtle.

Little brother was in tears as he reminded me, "He always gets to pick. I always have to do what he says. He's gonna keep the turtle in his room and make me pay him to see it."

Good grief. Two turtles, two aquariums, split the food and maybe I can still get a small drink. That was before we talked to the store owner, better known as the "take-mama-for-all-she's-got-turtle-lobbyist."

By the time we got out of there, I was lucky to still have my shirt. The slider had to have the aquarium starter kit complete with full-spectrum lighting, gravel, and a filter. The box turtle prefers a habitat lined with rabbit food and you must sprinkle vitamin supplements on its food. Oh, and don't forget the heated rock. Turtles need those, too. Throw in two books on keeping and breeding turtles in captivity and you begin to understand why the Legislature is allowing home equity loans.

As my children stood there ecstatically with their turtles in cute little boxes watching me search for a charge card that could handle this financial assault, I asked the turtle lady, "Is there a warranty on these creatures?"

"Yes ma'am, 14 days. If they die in 14 days, you get a full refund or a new turtle."

We've done everything by the book but that slider looks sick to me. My family says he's fine, but I know that sucker is dying. Today is the 14th day, and he's hanging on just to mess me over. Last night after the kids went to bed I told him, "Look buddy, just say the word and I can pull the plug. The warranty is almost up and if you're dying, don't feel like you have to hang on for our sakes. He's a strong kid. I'll get him a video, and he'll be fine. You just go on to turtle heaven so I can get my money back."

Nothing. He just looked at me with those gold eyes and pulled his head back into his shell. Then my son woke up and told me to stop pestering his turtle.

Well, he's got until 7 PM That's when the pet store closes. Stay tuned and pray for Tupac. I'll keep you posted.

Tupac is Dead

The turtle died.

For me, this is not as bad as the rabbit dying but it's a close second. As I write this, I am wearing black as a sign of mourning, and because I really need to do laundry.

You remember, Tupac, my son's turtle don't you? He was the red-eared slider turtle that I bought on credit three weeks ago. Well, he's six inches under now in the good shoe box that my suede pumps came in. Life really is a four-letter word isn't it?

I knew something was wrong with that turtle from the moment I saw him at the pet store. He had beady eyes, and he wouldn't make eye contact like the other turtles. He kind of weaved when he was swimming, too, like he was on something, you know. Anyway, I tried to get my son, Austin, to pick a box turtle like his brother but no he had to have a water turtle.

Water turtles need water and a bunch of other stuff that I won't be able to get rid of at a garage sale. We did everything for Tupac. That turtle got more attention than I did, and what thanks do we get? Two days after the guarantee was up, he lost his will to live.

The boys called me at work to tell me. Sure, I had noticed that Tupac looked a little odd that morning when I peeked in on my son before leaving for work, but then, I never thought he looked all that healthy. He was sprawled out on that heated rock like he'd been partying all night. I just kissed my son and went on my merry way.

My assistant called me to the phone later that day, even though I was quite busy. But I always take calls from my family.

My son said, "Mom, can I put ice cream on a peanut butter sandwich? The baby sitter said I could only put jelly."

"That's fine, son. Make sure you clean up the kitchen when you're done. Love ya, gotta go."

"OK," he said. Then almost as an after thought, he added, "Oh yeah, my turtle died. I think he killed himself."

Wonderful. We bought a suicidal turtle that I haven't even paid for yet.

"Son, I'm sorry about your turtle. I'm sure he didn't suffer and he's in a better place now. We'll have a little ceremony when I get home and bury him OK?"

"Well, can I do an autopsy and see what killed him?"

"Son, leave the turtle alone. Just put him in a box or something and wait for me or your father."

"Can I have a dog? Dogs swim better than turtles."

"Goodbye, son."

Strangely, I felt a great sense of loss with the demise of Tupac.

Could it be that I finally had formed an attachment to a non-homo sapien? Or could it be the astronomical interest rate accumulating on my credit card? Maybe it was just the loss of a really good shoebox. It's hard to say.

This I do know. The next pet I buy will be a Beanie Baby. No food, no filter, no fuss.

Turkey Thighs

Does anyone know what happened to Thanksgiving? I've looked all over the place for a sign of my favorite holiday and all I've come up with is leftover Halloween and premature Christmas.

Thanksgiving is such a simple holiday. There are no cards to mail or gifts to buy. All that's required is one day of eating like there's no tomorrow. Now, someone has gone and done away with it, and I didn't even get a memo or some sort of notice.

There are already Christmas decorations in the malls, and it's only the first week of November. I got my first Christmas card today. That is too much pressure. If I get my cards out before December 31, it's a good year for me. I want to do a photo card again for Christmas. Maybe I'll save some time and use the same one from last year. The kids didn't grow much this year and they still have those cute sweaters. I doubt that anyone would notice.

I think we're only a few days from Thanksgiving. I sure hope so. I must have the peace and simplicity of Thanksgiving. I must eat enough turkey and dressing to make me almost sick, but not quite.

Some of my fondest memories are of this holiday. There is no disappointment about getting the wrong gift or not getting any gifts. There are no firecrackers to explode in my hand before I can toss them into the air. There's nothing to buy but groceries. We simply spend a day with our family, eating like pigs and watching football.

My only sad Thanksgiving was in 1989. I'll never forget that one. That was the year that my inner thighs first met each other. Before that, there was no communication between them unless I crossed my legs. It was like being in the Twilight Zone. I finally forced myself to get up from the table after eating my second dessert. I took one step and my right thigh brushed against my left thigh. I was momentarily startled but I kept walking. My legs got into an argument as I walked.

"Hey, watch it buddy! Stop bumping into me."

"Look, girlfriend, I can't help it. She keeps sending more fat down here. Where am I supposed to put it all? The hips are already overcrowded so you'll probably be seeing a lot more of me."

"That's just great. All of this friction could start a fire in these cheap panty hose."

"Let's tell the feet to spread out a little and give us some room."

"That's a great idea."

They've been bosom buddies every since and I find that I don't trip as much since I started walking like a rodeo cowboy.

But even with that close encounter, I still want Thanksgiving to get its just due. The name alone is special. I can spare a few days to give thanks for the good times.

Hey! I just found Thanksgiving on two calendars so I guess we are having it after all. Parades, food, family! I love it. Let the good times roll. Who knows? My stomach might meet my lap this year.

Lawnmower Lessons

I learned something this weekend ~ which is a delightful change from the previous three weekends when I learned absolutely nothing. I learned that there is a right way and a wrong way to mow the yard.

Who knew?

I thought that it was sufficient to just chop down the giant weeds until they are even with the grass. I like that look. It works for me. Apparently, I was wrong.

Men do not simply cut the grass. They manicure the lawn. They style the earth's thick, green covering. They create masterpieces on soil using mere lawn tools. Like I said before: Who knew?

On Saturday, my husband went on a well-deserved fishing trip to Lake Texoma with some of his buddies. (He took no fishing equipment and he didn't bring any of the "one-hundred" fish they caught home. But that's another story.) Anyway, since our yard was looking like an Amazon rain forest, I decided to assume one of his routine household chores and mow the grass.

When I was girl, I cut the yard all of the time despite my severe allergies to grass and trees. I did it for the money. Youngsters do that sort of thing, you know.

I hate having the worst looking front yard on the street. It's the first thing I see when I get home each day. It's the first thing my neighbors see when they drive by. I don't care what the back yard looks like but I want the front yard to give the appearance that our home has not been deserted.

So on Saturday, I popped a non-drowsy formula antihistamine and proceeded to cut the grass in record time. I went up and down, back and forth, to, fro and around a few times. I even made an effort to get especially close to the curb and borders to save him some time with the weed eater later on.

I do not do the weed eater thing. I hate that contraption. It's too heavy and it smokes as it burns that stinky fuel. Plus, the fishing line flings grass clippings all over my socks and they get really dirty.

Sometimes when Honey Bunny cuts the grass, he doesn't get around to trimming the edges. Then I have to go out there with a pair of scissors and trim the grass along the curb. When someone drives by, I hide the scissors in the grass and pretend I'm pulling up weeds. Trimming the grass with scissors looks so neurotic. I only do this when we're expecting guests.

I was awfully proud of my final result. The yard looked magnificent except for two or three stubborn weeds that had defied the blade. I got my scissors and cut those and then the yard was perfect.

Imagine my surprise, when my husband came home and told me that I had butchered the yard!

I can handle criticism; goodness knows I've had enough of it in my lifetime. However, I was expecting his gratitude and compliments for my efforts. I told him that I was expecting a thank you not disparaging remarks. But he didn't feel like I had helped him at all. In fact, he informed me that he was going to have to "remow" the yard, immediately!

"Why couldn't you just leave the yard alone?" he asked. "I told you that I would take care of it when I got back."

Well, he also told me he was going to mow the yard five days before he left. I'm sure you can understand my impatience.

What madness is this? Why in the world would someone remow freshly cut grass?

We went outside so that he could show me exactly what he was talking about. Initially, all I saw was my good looking yard. Sure, there was no distinct pattern to the finished product; and yes, there were a few bald spots but overall, I thought it looked nice. It just needed to be edged up.

I was terribly wrong.

Honey Bunny pointed out that my neighbors all had very exacting, precise, and symmetric designs sculpted into their grass. David, across the street, has an interesting diagonal pattern while Tom, next door, seems to prefer the vertical cutting method. Our yard, on the other hand, appeared to have been cut by a drunk driver.

I told him that I had patterned the design after a jig saw puzzle to be different from the other lawns that all looked like fairways at The Masters or the outfield at the Ballpark in Arlington. He failed to see the humor in that remark.

Well, lions and tigers and bears, oh my. Big deal. The grass would grow out in a few days, just like a bad hair cut. Why remow it now?

"Follow me and don't say word," he ordered.

We went into the laundry room and he took a load of towels from the dryer. He then proceeded to fold them the way he had when we first got married. Next, he went into each bathroom and reversed all of the rolls of toilet tissue so that the tissue went under instead of over. Then, he stacked the dishwasher and put cups where the bowls should go! AAarrrggh! My hysteria grew with each stake he used to drive his point home to my heart.

Finally, he stopped tormenting me and said, "You're going to redo everything I just did as soon as we get through discussing this aren't you? Just like you rewash the dishes that the kids have already washed, after they go to bed. Just like you remake the guest bed after our company leaves. Just like..."

"OK. OK. I get the point. It does make a difference."

Who knew?

Walking Home From Work

Sometimes it seems like there are only evil people left in the world.

I'm ashamed to admit it but occasionally I just skip the world and local news. I just can't bear the emotions that accompany the endless stories about molestation, murders, and mayhem.

My mom used to warn me not to stare at people. I'd always ask her why not and she'd say, "Because they might be strange."

"Well that's why I'm looking at them," I'd explain.

Anyway, I'm pleased to report that I recently met some very nice strangers (and I was careful not to stare at them). Now, I believe there's hope for this planet after all.

Last month, my car was in the shop so my husband took me to work. I finished work early and since he wasn't due back for a couple of hours, I decided to walk home. It was only three miles and it was such a lovely day. I grabbed my brief case and headed out before anyone could stop me.

I had gone a couple of blocks down the busy boulevard when a nice man in a pickup pulled over and offered me a ride. He was very nice. He followed me for half a mile trying to persuade me to get into his car. It was an unseasonably warm day and I was enjoying being outdoors and getting some exercise. I kept saying, "No, thank you," but he wouldn't give up.

Finally, I just had to ask, "By the way, why are you wearing a ski mask and gloves?"

He mumbled something about a skin condition as he sped away. I hope I didn't hurt his feelings.

I had gone about a mile when I realized that I really wasn't dressed properly for a long walk. My feet hurt and that briefcase felt like a 50 lb. dumbbell. Then along came a friendly lady with her rowdy quintuplets.

"Do you wanna go bye-bye?" she asked me.

She obviously hadn't had a conversation with another adult in a long time.

"Thanks but I'm almost home," I lied.

"What was that?" she asked over the screams from the back of the minivan.

"No, thank you!"

"OK," she said, "Mommy go now."

I was starting to feel like Kung Fu walking across the desert when I spotted a convenience store ahead. I raced towards it, but it was only a mirage. I was standing in the middle of someone's yard when I came to my senses. Their dog chased me for six blocks.

I was sitting on the curb panting when a friendly toddler rolled up to me on his tricycle.

"Watcha doing?" he lisped through the space where his front teeth once resided.

"I'm walking home."

"I'll give you a ride, but I can only go to the end of the street," he offered.

"That's OK. I can make it."

"Are you strange? I'm not s'posed to talk to strange people."

"I'm not strange, I'm eccentric."

"Oh."

I was three blocks from home when my husband pulled up and said, "Hey babe, hop in. Your receptionist called me and told me you were trying to walk home."

"Trying to walk home? I can spit in our yard from here."

"OK," he said and drove off laughing. He only went a few yards and stopped. People stared at me as I ran after him screaming.

Maybe I am strange. Oh well.

Weather Mom

I am the official weather lady for my family. Each morning, at precisely 7 AM, I announce the weather forecast to my family. You must be very specific and fairly accurate in an important position like this one.

"Boys," I say, "the windows feel cold. You should wear a coat today. And take your umbrellas, too; my shoulder is aching so it's going to rain."

Immediately the whining begins.

"Aw, mom, we don't need coats! Nobody ever wears a coat but us. All the other kids wear shorts and T-shirts unless it snows."

We see more comets than snow in Texas, but I ignore his distorted remark and reply, "Then you will be the only kids at your school to survive the flu season. Won't that be wonderful?"

"But Mom the last time we wore coats it got up to 70 degrees, and I almost melted at recess," my oldest son reminds me.

"Well son, that was my mistake. I'd watched the news and they'd predicted a cold front. I should have just stuck my hand outside to check the weather. This time I'm positive. Dress warmly."

They still remember those cold winters when we lived up north. Back then, we thought 40 degrees Fahrenheit was picnic weather. The temperature had to reach the teens before you would even hear anyone use the word "cold." During the Halloween Blizzard of '91, it got so cold that they issued a warning to people from the South to stay indoors. Some lady from Alabama went outside to shovel her driveway, and she instantly exploded into a million icicles. They say the neighborhood smelled like magnolias for weeks after that happened.

Anyway, almost invariably, one of my sons appears for breakfast wearing shorts and a sweater. "Son," I ask, "why aren't you wearing long pants?"

"These shorts are warm Mom. They're corduroy."

"And where did you get those shoes. I didn't buy those."

"I traded with Adriel. He liked my shoes better."

I understand why when I survey the faded canvas shoes with the shredded shoe strings. Finally, I say, "Do not come home without your own shoes or else." Vague but menacing, that's a pretty good threat, I guess.

Meanwhile, I forget about the shorts until I pick him up from school and he says, "My teacher said it's too cold to wear shorts to school."

I sigh and ask him, "Where are your shoes?"

"Oh, Adriel didn't wear them today, but he says they're in good shape."

"Where's your brother?"

"He's looking in the 'lost and found' for his coat."

With a clap of thunder, the skies open up and a downpour begins. My other child races to the car dragging his coat on the ground behind him. He climbs into the back seat grinning from ear to ear. He tosses a muddy bundle onto the car seat. "Look Mom, I found my brother's shoes!"

I smile, adjust my windshield wipers, turn up the heater, and drive home.

Super Bowl Fan

Ladies and gentleman, I'm going out on a limb today to challenge an archaic myth concerning the proper behavior of sports fans. It's scary crawling out to the end of this brittle twig just to espouse an opposing point of view, because I've been out here before and - I fell off.

Let me begin at the beginning. Last Sunday, one of the biggest sporting events of the year took place in Miami. Super Bowl XXXIII, the disappointing matchup between the dirty birds of Atlanta and the unbeatable Broncos of Denver, lasted two quarters too long and ended with the Broncos winning their second championship in a row.

We hosted our annual Super Bowl Party. We invited several friends over and as usual, the room was evenly divided in loyalties. The Falcon fans, including myself, sat on one side of the room and the Bronco fans were assigned to the other side, the side with the worst view of the television. During the first quarter, my side was exuberant. The underdogs from down South played well and us Falcon Fans were happy.

In the second quarter, the tide began to shift a bit as the Broncos came charging back down the field under the direction of General Elway. The game went into half time with a big question mark over the final outcome.

Well, midway into the third quarter, it was clear to me that the Falcons were a sinking ship. As I am not a captain, I felt no compulsion to go down with them so I changed teams.

"I'm cheering for Denver now," I announced during a commercial break.

I probably should have told everyone my decision during the game since the commercials were a lot more interesting by this point. After a minute or two, my words finally sank in and, by golly, all heck broke loose.

"You can't do that!" my husband yelled. "You can't change teams in the middle of the game."

"Why not?"

"It's, it's, it's un-American! You're supposed to have some loyalty to your team. You stand by them in good times and bad. You can't just abandon them every time they get down a few points." Everyone was nodding in agreement and looking at me like I had set off the alarm in a department store entryway.

"Look," I said, "I just picked Atlanta to be nice. I've been cheering for Minnesota all year and this would have been a better game if they had played in it. I don't even know the Falcons. The running back's name is Anderson like mine so I picked the Falcons. I hardly think that means a commitment for life. Besides Elway has such great teeth and I used to live in Terrell when I was kid. Doesn't that count for something?"

Their expressions didn't change but at least the Denver fans moved over so I could sit down. In the end, my team won and I was happy. Sure, if I was actually on the team or if I had a personal interest in the team, it would be a different story. I would fight, cheer, or lobby to the end on their behalf. But professional football is simply entertainment whether the fat lady sings or not.

So I'll never make the All-Madden team as "best fan in the NFL." That's okay. I sort of like it out here, all by myself, on a limb.

Willie The Kid

It was sundown on the prairie. I placed a hand above my brow and squinted toward the western horizon. The dying rays of the fireball made long shadows accompany the cowpokes strolling down Main Street. I sighed and wiped my hands on my apron for the hundredth time.

Where is that kid the folks call Willie, I wondered aloud. He said that he'd return long before the Harvest Moon peeped over Twobucks Ridge. I'd been watching and waiting for half an hour but there was nary a sign of that man-child. Just as I turned to head back into the saloon, a cloud of dust appeared among the cacti occupying the desert on the outskirts of town.

Then, I heard ole One-Boot Kevin yell at the top of his lungs, "He's coming! The Kid is back!"

The sheriff fired his pistol into the air six times. It could have been a warning but then again; maybe he was just excited about his new gun. Either way, folks grabbed their younguns and headed indoors in a hurry. I, too, deserted the dusty road. Not that I was afraid of Willie, but that half-blind horse of his was a bit unpredictable.

I was behind the bar fixing a sarsaparilla when The Kid strolled through the flapping doors. He paused, and looked around the room. The piano grew quiet and everyone froze. In the corner, the drifter known as Nobody let out an eerie whistle and retreated beneath his pancho like a turtle in a stampede. Somebody Jones laughed, but he hasn't been right since The Kid's horse kicked him in the ear last year. The rest of us kept our eyes on The Kid.

The kid looked at me and tipped his hat. Then he blinked his right eye three times and said, "Evening, Ma."

"Evening, Kid," I replied. "I'll have your supper right out."

He made his way to the back of the room and sat down at the table with his brother, Sillie. Sillie grunted but didn't speak.

Safe for now, everyone resumed their conversations and card games. The piano man played a happy tune. A breeze came through the door bringing the odor of horse flesh and cow patties. All was well.

I came out of the kitchen carrying two plates. I placed one in front of The Kid and one in front of Sillie. They bowed their heads briefly and then Sillie picked up his fork.

"Wait!" shouted The Kid.

Once again, everyone froze.

The Kid reached for his holster, and we gasped in unison. I started trembling as he slowly withdrew his ~ ruler. He measured Sillie's piece of Texas toast and then he measured his own. Mercifully, they were the same dimensions. Then he pulled out a meat scale from his boot and weighed the wieners. All was equal. But then, he began to count the beans.

"No, son. Don't do it," I pleaded. "You're just gonna make yourself upset. I promise you, it's all evenly distributed. Besides, all those beans together don't amount to a hill. Please, Kid, just eat. Why torture yourself like this?"

"It's the principle of the thing, Mama," he said. "You say that you love us the same, but you always give my brother a little more food than me. He gets the biggest cookie. He gets a larger slice of cake. Last week, he had half an ounce more water than me in his bubble bath."

"But, Kid, he's two years older than you and sixty pounds heavier! Come on, Kid, you're not a bean counter. Stop the madness. You know that I love you, boy."

But the Kid just kept counting those beans. In the corner, some ranch hands were placing bets on the outcome of our family feud. I couldn't stand by and see my family torn apart over something so trivial.

Finally, in desperation, I said, "Kid, if you love me. You'll stop this nonsense and eat your supper."

The Kid looked at me. Then he put down his magnifying glass and glared at his brother. Slowly, he picked up his fork and started to eat those cold beans.

I looked up and thanked my lucky stars. We'd survived another close one on the range.

Destiny, My Neighbor

Like a rabbit in a magician's top hat, he suddenly appeared one day. We had been in our new home all of six hours when I heard the doorbell ring. I went to the door expecting a delivery man. Our old mattress was so worn and pathetic that I was too embarrassed to risk our new neighbors seeing it and thinking bad things about us.

I looked through the peephole and, seeing no one, assumed that I was mistaken about the sound I'd heard. I was walking away when a soft rap penetrated the hard wood. I opened the door and there he was, a little fellow who barely cleared my kneecaps.

"I'm Tevin," he said. Pointing to a house across the street, he added, "I live over there. Do you have any kids?"

"Yes,Tevin, we have two children."

"Are they any good?" he asked with a frown.

"I think they're pretty good. They get in trouble sometimes but..."

"No," he interrupted, "I mean are they boys? We don't need no more girls on this street."

I chuckled and replied, "We have two boys and one of them is about your age. Let me get them for you. Maybe you can show them around the neighborhood."

I left him by the front door but when I came back he was in the kitchen drinking our last juice box. That was my first clue that we'd be seeing a lot more of Tevin.

Every day for the rest of that summer, Tevin appeared at our front door at dawn. We tried to explain to him that visiting hours don't start until 10:00 am but he didn't believe us. Eventually, he became like another son to us. If he didn't show up for dinner, I worried.

"Where's Tevin? Dinner is ready and I made his favorite meal, spaghetti."

"He went home for dinner."

"You mean, he doesn't live here? Do they even know what he

likes to eat? Maybe I should call them; milk gives him gas you know."

We took him to the circus and the zoo with us. We applauded his good report cards. We worried when he had the flu. It's amazing how someone unrelated to you can become such an important part of your life.

A few days ago, a big, yellow moving van pulled up in front of Tevin's house and we watched sadly as they transported our friends away. I couldn't bring myself to say goodbye to Tevin. It was just too hard.

The next day when the doorbell rang, I rushed to answer it. Momentarily forgetting the events of the preceding day, I assumed that Tevin had lost his key again. I was surprised to find a lovely young girl about the age of my oldest son standing at the threshold.

"Hello ma'am. I'm Destiny, your new neighbor. Someone told me that you have a son about my age, and I was hoping that he could introduce me to the other kids in the neighborhood."

My heart beat wildly as something alien possessed me and made me say, "No dear, I'm sorry but we don't have any children." I quickly closed the door when I heard my oldest son coming down the stairs.

"Who was that mom?" he inquired.

Destiny.

Aversion to Affection

Whew! I am worn out. I have exhausted my last bit of energy in a fruitless marathon that yielded no tangible results. In the end, I am left forlorn and uttering the same question that mothers have asked themselves for countless generations, "Why won't my son let me kiss him?"

It all started this morning when my oldest son who refers to himself as "almost-a-teenager" came into the kitchen to prepare his lunch for school. I was drinking my ritual morning cup of coffee and scanning the headlines.

I watched him as he reached up to the top shelf of the pantry for peanut butter. For the first time, I noticed that he didn't have to tip toe or use a chair to get to that shelf. Then he took a knife and spread the peanut butter smoothly across the bread without punching a hole in it. He even cleaned the knife off when he was done. He placed everything into a paper bag and put it in his backpack. I was so proud of him. My little man can dress himself, make his bed, and prepare his own lunch. My, my haven't we come a long way, I thought.

My heart swelled with pride, and I walked over to him intent on giving him a big hug and a kiss on the cheek. He saw me coming toward him and immediately recognized my maternal expression.

"Mom, stop!" he said. "I don't want a kiss. It's too early to kiss people."

I grinned and lunged for him anyway. He took off like the Roadrunner with Wile E. Coyote chasing him. I was full of caffeine, so I figured that I could catch him. Boy, is that kid fast! He circled the kitchen table a few times before he headed toward the den where he leapt over the sofa in a single bound.

I remained close on his heels as he ran to his room. He tried to slam the door but I was just quick enough to get a foot in. We ran around and over the obstacles scattered about his room until I penned him on one side of his bed with his back against the wall.

His eyes flitted from right to left frantically.

"Please mom! I don't want a kiss. How about I just give you $10 to go away?"

When I simply smiled in response, he yelled, "Dad, help me! Mom is trying to kill me!"

"Son, a simple kiss from your mother won't kill you," I said. You'd have died years ago if that was the case. You used to let me kiss you all the time on your fat little cheeks. And you'd kiss me back, too."

"Mom, that was a hundred years ago. I'm a man now. Men don't like to kiss."

I leaned across the bed certain of victory. To my surprise, he did a four-foot vertical leap, stepped on my back, and ran out of the room. I followed him outside and chased him down the street. He ran into a neighbor's back yard and startled their turkey who was trying to dial the SPCA on a cell phone with his beak. Just then, his father pulled up in his truck, threw open the passenger door, and yelled, "Come on son! She's slowing down! You can make it."

Outnumbered, outmaneuvered, and outcast, I watched in silence as he ran and dove into the truck. His father sped away before the door was shut.

That's OK. He'll be back. I'm sure of it.

I have his lunch.

Recycling

I have nothing against kids going outside of the box. I've been out there and it's pretty scary. Why not let the young and brave do some exploring?

I only have a problem when they come back into my box, inside my walls, with a superiority complex. I really don't need someone who goes to bed before the news comes on telling me how to live my life.

Still they persist in bringing me the latest news flashes from the outside world. Now, I'm getting a lesson on recycling.

"Mom, we have to start doing a better job of recycling," my son informed me a few days ago. "I know your generation didn't do a lot of recycling, but if we want to save the ozone and the rainforest, we have to consume less and preserve more."

I just stared at him over the rim of my coffee cup. I have trouble forming sentences before I have my coffee so he picked a great time for this lesson.

"See Mom. We can't put everything in one paper bag like we've been doing. We need to separate the plastic from the newspaper. We should also have a container for the aluminum. We can even recycle the foil because it can be melted down and made into something useful."

He paused and waited for me to respond with awe and wonder.

I just stared at him.

"Mom, are you listening? Have you gone to that Mommy place in your mind again where women get pedicures and eat chocolate all day?

"No son," I said. "I was just thinking about how much you remind me of your great-grandmother."

"Did she recycle too? I didn't think they knew about recycling back in the olden days."

"Son, my grandmother invented recycling. The only things she ever threw out were bones for the dogs and she made soup with those before they got to them. She had the skinniest dogs I've ever seen."

I put my empty coffee cup on the table and leaned back in my chair.

"Now you must remember that your great-grandmother lived through the Depression and three or four wars so she knew how to make it through hard times. Grandma could stretch a dollar so far that even George Washington would tell a fib just to get out of her tight fist.

Listen, I remember one family reunion when I had to carry the same cup around for three days because grandma wouldn't give us another one. It was a plastic cup for goodness sake! To grandma, plastic didn't mean disposable, it just meant that we wouldn't break it when we washed it.

Every blue moon, she would buy that wonderful Blackburn's Syrup from the manufacturing plant right there in Jefferson, Texas where she lived. Once the syrup was gone, and it took a while, because she poured it for us, she would use the thick glass jars that the syrup came in to store her fruit preserves.

After we ate the preserved fruit and vegetables in the winter, we used those same jars to drink water drawn from her well in the summer. Of course, once she discovered plastic, she saved the good jars for company.

Grandma didn't waste a thing. She read the paper from cover to cover, then she used it to wrap our Christmas presents or to start the fire in her wood burning stove. And forget melting the aluminum; we had to wash that too! Grandma reused a piece of foil until it tarnished and turned into paper.

Boy, that woman was resourceful. The most amazing thing she ever did was to save the cotton balls from all of her aspirin bottles and knit me a sweater before I went off to college."

At this point, my son looks a little skeptical. "Mom, did she really knit you a sweater from cotton balls?"

"OK. I made that part up but the rest of the story is true. See there's this old saying about necessity being the mother of invention. Well, your grandmother didn't start recycling to save the planet; she did it so that her large family could survive. I guess I'd sort of forgotten all those wonderful lessons she taught me about not wasting anything and being content with what you have.

Thanks for reminding me son."

"Sure, Mom, no problem. But we need to talk about the computer too. You haven't been shutting it down properly and–"

"OK, son. Let's talk about that tomorrow. I can only absorb one lecture a day. I from those olden days, you know. We're kind of slow."

Need more copies? Or Send one to a friend.

Send him or her *Mom, Are We There Yet?*

Monica Anderson
4101 W. Green Oaks Boulevard, Suite 305, #174
Arlington, Texas 76016

Email: Moe@MoeAnderson.com
Web Site: www.MoeAnderson.com

Or ask for it at your favorite bookstore or library!

TO:

_____
NAME

_____
ADDRESS

_____
CITY, STATE, ZIP CODE   *Every copy autographed.*

FROM:

_____
NAME

_____
ADDRESS

_____
CITY, STATE, ZIP CODE

$12.95 x (Quantity)	$
Tax *(Texas Residents Add 7.75%)*	
Shipping & Handling	$3.00
Total Amount Due:	$

Check or Money Order to: Monica Anderson
Please allow two weeks for delivery.

About the Author

A native of Texas, Monica Frazier Anderson
is a freelance columnist, dentist, and television talk-show host.
She is also the author of *Black English Vernacular: From Ain't to
Yo Mama.* She lives in Arlington, Texas with her husband, Alfred,
and their two sons.